The Beatles In Cleveland

Beatlemania swept across North America when John Lennon, Paul McCartney, George Harrison and Ringo Starr appeared on *The Ed Sullivan Show* in February 1964. The decade of the 1960's seemed to change overnight from black and white to color as a generation fell under the influence of the group's music, style and personalities.

Hot on the success of their film *A Hard Day's Night*, the Beatles 1964 summer tour filled auditoriums with screams of delight and excitement – and in some cases, full-blown fan hysteria. This was the case on September 15th in Cleveland, Ohio when police stopped the show in mid-performance and ordered the Beatles off the stage. The next year, they were banned from appearing in the city.

In August 1966, the group launched their final tour, but the innocence portrayed in *A Hard Day's Night* only two years earlier was missing. Controversy raging over Lennon's remarks about Christianity and the group being more popular than Jesus made their safety more of a concern than ever before.

A scheduling change brought the Beatles back to Cleveland on August 14th for the tour's first outdoor show at Municipal Stadium. The results were the same, but on a much larger scale. It was obvious they could no longer be protected in front of audiences and the first murmurings were overheard that it would be the last tour. This is an account of both these special moments in time: two of the wildest, out-of-control concerts in Beatle - and rock – history.

"One of the top cultural events in Cleveland history and one of the most exciting days in my nearly 30 years as a Plain Dealer rock critic." - **Jane Scott**.

"At Cleveland Municipal Stadium, the goal was to actually *touch* a Beatle." – **Jerry G. Bishop**, Cleveland radio and TV personality.

"Paul McCartney thought the show was cancelled, because it had been. So if he reads this book, it'll be a revelation for Sir Paul." – **Harry Martin**, Radio Television Broadcasters Hall of Fame of Ohio.

THE BEATLES IN CLEVELAND

Memories, Facts & Photos About
The Notorious 1964 & 1966 Concerts

Dave Schwensen

North Shore Publishing
Vermilion, OH

Dedication

To my mom Arlys and dad Eddie for taking me to see The Beatles in Cleveland on August 14, 1966 – and buying the EXPENSIVE seats!!

The Buddy System

To my cousin Johnny Moes and pal Kevin Murphy for attending this momentous occasion with me. Hey, are we still cool for being there or what??!!!

The Family

To Debbie, Kevin, Paul, Blake & Brooke for your humor, inspiration – and for keeping your hands off my Beatles stuff!

North Shore Publishing
P.O. Box 318
Vermilion, OH 44089

First Edition: April 2007

ISBN 978-0-9791030-0-1
Library of Congress Control Number: 2006938459

Schwensen, Dave.
  The Beatles In Cleveland / Dave Schwensen
Includes Index
Printed in the United States of America

Cover Design: Dave Schwensen

Cover Photo: The Beatles in Cleveland *today* on display at the Rock and Roll Hall of Fame and Museum – Cleveland, OH. Poster photo reproduced courtesy of the owner, Pete Howard.

CONTENTS

Act One

Act Two

THANK YOU

The influence of the Beatles should never be underestimated. Their impact on music, society and history ignited the 1960's and continues to this day. It's a safe bet to say your children's grandchildren will know of The Beatles.

How the group will be experienced by future generations is unknown, but for my purposes in putting together this book, the Internet has been invaluable. Through the online magic of posting a simple one page review about their August 14, 1966 concert on my business website at **thecomedybook.com**, I was exposed to a whole new world of information about the event. To my surprise, dedicated Beatle fans found the article and sent messages encouraging me to write more about what it was *really* like to see the Beatles live. Since it was a topic I'd always enjoyed talking about, it was not a problem putting my memories into words.

Eventually my article grew to the point where it deserved a website of its own and **beatlesincleveland.com** was launched. Each day brought the anticipation of an email containing another shared memory, lost photo, or lead for an important new contact. The website became the basis for this book and inspired my research.

I especially want to thank everyone included in this book. To say our conversations and emails have been "fab" and "gear" would be an understatement. I also want to give a special thanks to my new online friends who went beyond the call of duty with their help:

Wojciech (Wojtek) Borkowski, Brian Luoma, John McEwen, Joe Viglione, Chuck Gunderson, Bobbie Laughman, Craig Cemak, Ray Glasser, Jim Davison, Bob Becker, Dan Nainan, (my NYC computer guru), Patti Luchsinger, (my Ohio computer guru), and The Cleveland Memory Project.

Of course this book would not have been possible without John, Paul, George and Ringo. Thank you for writing and performing the soundtrack for our generation and many others to come.

And finally, for my son Paul, someday you'll read this and understand…

FOREWORD

When we booked John, Paul, George and Stuart for our art college dances, I can't remember them having a specific name. I just referred to them as "the college band." Images come back to me of them performing on the stage at the end of the canteen, being with them in the room behind the stage, and Stuart showing me his new bass guitar. These are fleeting images. The details of our conversations and of their performances at the dances have long since escaped me.

Virginia and I must have seen around two hundred performances by the Beatles, from their gigs in the cellar of the Jacaranda, to the Litherland Town Hall and Aintree Institute appearances. We were at most of their lunchtime, evening and all-night sessions at the Cavern, and were with them for the Royal Iris trips up the Mersey, all their Tower Ballroom gigs, and those at virtually every venue on Merseyside; Floral Hall, Southport; Queens Hall, Widnes; Plaza St Helens, and even their single appearance at the Locarno Ballroom in West Derby Road.

We saw them with Stuart, we saw them with Pete, and we saw them with Ringo. In those days, for a period of five years, Virginia and I would be out for lunchtime and evening sessions by the group, seven days a week.

As their fame grew, Virginia and I accompanied them on their first radio sessions in Manchester and their debut TV shows at Granada Television. During their tours we'd hang around with them backstage at venues such as the Ardwick, Apollo and ABC, Blackpool.

But, regretfully, we never saw them in Hamburg or America.

The audiences we had been part of were always electric; we'd feel the hair rise on the backs of our necks. They were compact audiences, squeezed tight in the Cavern or the Cassanova Club, or appearing in a larger venue such as the Tower Ballroom, which still radiated their power on stage. But even their theatre gigs before audiences of up to 1,200 people per house couldn't match the vast audiences of thousands in America.

I often wondered what they would be like. And now I know.

Dave Schwensen has focused this book on two shows in Cleveland: the 1964 appearance at Public Hall and 1966 at Municipal Stadium. He has produced an amazing contribution to Beatles history, spending three years interviewing the people who interacted with the Beatles on those occasions and playing detective to unearth every single particle of information surrounding those exciting events experienced by the fortunate fans in Cleveland who were able to attend.

So now I know what it was really like. I'm able to experience, somewhat vicariously, the fervor of the occasion, which makes Dave's book quite unique.

Although I documented the Mersey scene week by week, I was never able to document one specific gig in such detail. The stories of the Cleveland concerts are presented here in three dimensions - an exploration of an occasion experienced by the promoters, journalists and disc jockeys, fellow musicians, and fans. It's an incredible sharing of information by the people who were actually there.

As John Lennon once said "You had to be there." Well, Dave has created the nearest thing to actually witnessing the Cleveland concerts and it's a worthwhile contribution to the growing canon of works about the greatest rock group of them all. Thanks Dave, for lovingly compiling such an invaluable collection of memories.

Bill Harry.
Founder of Mersey Beat
www.mersey-beat.com

PREFACE
It Was 40 Years Ago Today

It wasn't exactly deja vu, or at least how I've come to understand the term. There were no feelings of having once before lived this exact moment in time, or watching a dream magically come to life before my eyes. Instead, a better description would be similar to a chance meeting between old friends as a result of being in the right place at the right time. The only difference was that my meeting occurred with a memory that had been lost for too long, but not forgotten.

I was surprised at how clear my recollection was of this one particular moment, considering it had only been a brief distraction on the way to a much larger, more chaotic, and unforgettable event. But the impression it had made on my once-teenaged mind was strong enough to be remembered four decades later. All it took was a chance meeting of weather, music, and a lonely voice of protest.

I was driving alone on a Saturday afternoon through an area of Cleveland called the West Side Market. It was early August, but instead of the usual summer heat and humidity that hangs over northern Ohio like a Lake Erie-powered sauna, the air was unseasonably chilly and damp. The sky was dark with heavy clouds and the rhythmic sweep of wipers across the car windshield pushed away a light rain that had been falling since morning.

In front of brick buildings I'd passed by so often they were not much more than background scenery, parked cars narrowed traffic lanes along West 25th Street and gave me an opportunity at each stop light to practice the fine art of people-watching. Despite the weather and a few impatient drivers practicing the fine art of people-dodging, shoppers crossed the street and filled the sidewalks searching for bargains. Many carried umbrellas and wore light jackets, while others simply ignored the rain, determined not to let it dampen the afternoon's outdoor activities.

Feeling the need for a musical soundtrack to discourage any possibility of a damp mood inside my car, I reached for a copy of The Beatles' *Revolver* and slid it into the CD player. Hitting the fast forward button, I found the opening notes of *Good Day Sunshine*, which any seasoned Beatles fan will recognize as the first song on the second side of the album released in August 1966.

For the unseasoned, an album was a vinyl, twelve-inch disk with grooves requiring a turntable and needle to be heard. For an added dose of sarcastic wit, this piece of equipment was often referred to as a record player. Since an album had two sides, it needed to be turned over to hear all the songs. These relics of the pop music culture were stored in cardboard sleeves and over the years some of the more creatively designed covers on these sleeves became valued for the artwork, as well as for the music inside. *Revolver* is a classic example of both.

Now that I've finished the humorous portion of *Introduction To Albums 101*, it's worth noting the second side of *Revolver*, beginning with *Good Day Sunshine*, has a personal history of chasing away any summertime blues that can be brought on by cold and damp weather. But the reason I'm bringing this up now, during my story about a drive in August 2006, will be made as clear as a cloudless sky over Lake Erie a bit later.

Since I wasn't interested in people-dodging or drawing attention from the Cleveland Police, I stopped for another red light. Glancing across the intersection at a corner park, I saw about a half dozen small, open-sided white tents forming a temporary outdoor flea market and protection from the rain. Each tent had tables displaying watches, clothes, souvenirs, and other items priced low enough to keep shoppers out of the drier stores. Apparently the bargains were worth braving the weather, because a large crowd had gathered in the park with more people heading in that direction.

Over the Beatles' harmony on *Good Day Sunshine*, a voice caught my attention. Glancing toward a building across from the park, I saw an older man wearing a dark suit standing on the corner next to a wooden box displaying two stacks of pamphlets or flyers. His pale-skinned face was topped by slicked-back short hair, and he was holding a sign that said "Jesus Saves" in big block letters. In his other hand, he grasped a megaphone to his mouth in an effort to make his religious message heard above the noise on the street.

Whether it was curiosity or just plain fate, I rolled down the car window to get a better view. Feeling the wet, chilly air on my face, I listened to the man's warnings for anyone who didn't repent his sins and follow a path of righteousness. At the same time I also watched shoppers pass him on their way to the flea market bargains, almost as if he didn't exist at all. In the background, side two of *Revolver* continued to play...

Suddenly, all the elements of that chance meeting stirred memories from forty years earlier. Sights, sounds and most importantly, feelings and emotions came rushing in through the open car window. My thoughts were swept back to another damp and chilly summer evening when I had watched a lone protester shouting a similar message at a crowd of people hurrying past him and toward a different event. In my mind it was August 14, 1966 all over again - and The Beatles were in Cleveland.

Act One

BACK BEAT OF TWO CITIES AND A STADIUM

Located on what residents refer to as The North Coast of The United States, Cleveland, Ohio, has often been compared to England's seaport of Liverpool. Both cities have diverse populations, a shared reliance on shipping, and were built around important rivers: The Cuyahoga and The Mersey. Stone, brick and concrete buildings darkened by factory smoke formed the surrounding urban landscapes, while strong muscles and seasoned characters supplied the manpower to make it all work.

To sailors on The Great Lakes, the area where The Cuyahoga flows into Lake Erie is still known as The Port of Cleveland. The river serves as a line dividing the city into an East Side and West Side, which are connected by a series of bridges that are either built high, or able to rise or rotate when cargo freighters are navigating to various upriver loading docks.

The low-lying district where the lake and river meet is known as The Flats. A focal point of the shipping industry for over 150 years, The Flats had developed a reputation by the 1960's as an area to avoid. Docks and bars attracted a tougher crowd, criminal activity was not unheard of, and the atmosphere of dirt, grime, soot and smoke cast a dark shadow over the Lake Erie coastline. When pollution caused a section of The Cuyahoga to burst into flames in June 1969, a stream of international headlines and endless jokes influenced Federal and State Legislators to pass laws aimed at cleaning-up The Great Lakes and its tributaries.

After massive renovations in the 1980's, The Flats now boasts a successful reputation for urban progress and has become a popular center for entertainment and nightlife. Restaurants, clubs, an outdoor concert stage and high-profile family events attract visitors, while future plans include luxury condos and permanent dockage for pleasure boats.

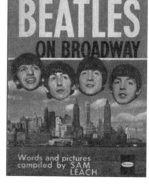

Rising up on higher ground next to the river is downtown Cleveland. With The Flats attracting people and dollars from the suburbs, investors continued the revamping of the city with a new baseball stadium, sports arena, Science Center, and renovation of the Playhouse Square District, which is second only to New York City's Broadway in the number of theaters located in one area.

On the lakefront at the northern edge of downtown is The Rock and Roll Hall of Fame and Museum. Though other cities competed to be the permanent location, Cleveland was chosen for a number of reasons.

The term "rock'n roll" was broadcast in 1951 for the first time – ever – by local radio disc jockey, Allen Freed, over northern Ohio airwaves. The city is also credited with hosting the first rock'n roll concert, Freed's *Moondog Coronation Ball* in March, 1952. And finally, Cleveland was the overwhelming favorite to host the pop culture icon in a poll by readers of the nationally syndicated newspaper, *USA Today*. The innovative architecture of the building was designed to include support beams over Lake Erie and for many fans solidifies a musical bond between the seaports of Cleveland and Liverpool:

Cleveland is the home of rock'n roll. Liverpool is the home of the most influential rock'n roll group the world has ever known, The Beatles.

West of the The Rock Hall, as it's commonly known, is Cleveland Browns Stadium. Home of the city's National Football League team, the giant structure opened in 1999 and was built on the same site where an even more massive outdoor arena once stood:

Cleveland Municipal Stadium.

Constructed primarily for baseball in 1931, Municipal Stadium could seat over 80,000 people. In fact, it was the setting for the first ever *Monday Night Football* telecast in 1970 when more than 85,000 fans cheered the local Browns over The New York Jets.

Except for the centerfield bleachers, the grayish-blue stadium had two seating decks covered by a partial roof, surrounding the playing field. Iron support beams for the roof and upper deck were spaced throughout the seating areas and would block the view for any unlucky ticket holders who had a seat behind one. Because of the expansive area within the stadium, the playing fields for both baseball and football were quite a distance from the nearest seats. For fans hoping to get a closer look at any on-field action, binoculars were an important piece of equipment. Behind the bleachers was a large, manually-operated scoreboard used to keep track of the Cleveland team's game, other games, display advertisements, and in the days long before computerized graphics, flash simple messages in white lights over a black background to the crowd.

The stadium, like The Rock Hall, sat near the lake and offered scenic views of the water and downtown skyline. But its location also made it a victim of the unpredictable northern Ohio weather. With Lake Erie being the shallowest of The Great Lakes, storms could build up force quickly and turn a beautiful summer day at the stadium into an experience of driving wind and rain without much warning.

It was here, within the over-sized proportions of Cleveland Municipal Stadium on a chilly, wet, and windy night in August 1966, that the home of rock'n roll played host to the most influential rock'n roll group the world has ever known. The result was one of the wildest, out-of-control concerts in Beatle - and rock – history.

FROM BLACK & WHITE TO COLOR

By the spring of 1966, Beatlemania was well into its third year as a cultural phenomenon in The United States. Since their debut on *The Ed Sullivan Show* in February 1964, John Lennon, Paul McCartney, George Harrison and Ringo Starr had dominated the American music charts and taken the concept of rock'n roll concerts from small theaters and music halls, into the realm of mass adoration held in sports arenas and outdoor stadiums.

The Beatles' performance at New York's Shea Stadium on August 15, 1965 had shattered attendance records that had once only been newsworthy for major sporting events. In just over two years they had changed not only the technology and production concepts needed for large scale performances, but also the sound of popular music and how it was presented to the public. Their image and unique personalities displayed a youthful element of fun to a country reeling under a president's assassination, threats of nuclear weapons, Cold War, the Vietnam War, racial conflicts, and a generation of teenaged baby-boomers searching for an identity to call their own. The Beatles' influence went well beyond music and affected many aspects of society including fashion, film, television, and attitudes - regardless of what generation you happened to be part of.

A devoted fan base of teenagers and pre-teens had embraced the Beatles' creativity, opinions, and style. Baby-boomers had matured along with the group and were moving beyond the idea of being "cool," which best described Elvis and James Dean in the 1950's. By

1966, it was more relevant to be "groovy" and "hip." The next year's Summer of Love was already simmering in San Francisco and London, and American youth was only three years away from becoming The Woodstock Generation.

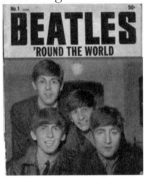

The Beatles were Great Britain's most famous export of the 1960's, but went far beyond the boundaries of free trade. Their carefully protected image as four care-free, long-haired lads in matching suits from Liverpool may have been shocking to the older generation at first, but adult morals gradually considered The Mop Tops safer for teenage admiration than the scruffier-looking groups who followed during the next wave of the British Music Invasion.

"Would you let your daughter marry a Rolling Stone?" asked a brilliant piece of promotion for the longer-haired rockers fronted by a pouting Mick Jagger and scowling Brian Jones. With the devilish Keith Richards lurking in the background, it's no wonder parents looked at the accompanying photo and preferred the idea of Ringo Starr sitting at the dinner table next to their young daughters.

The Beatles had grown to represent the youth of the world with a string of hit songs and albums that instinctively conveyed and stirred their fans' innermost feelings and emotions. Screaming girls and envious boys filled arenas and made Beatle tours of North America, Europe, Asia, and Australia closer to events than concerts. The films *A Hard Day's Night* and *Help!* carried the excitement to movie theaters in even the smallest towns, while extensive media coverage made them frequent household guests through television, radio, newspapers and magazines.

Even countries where governments banned any mention of the group, fearing their joyful sense of independence and irreverence would inspire rebellion, (or at the very least, teenaged lust), could not

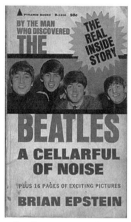

completely block their influence. What this censorship actually achieved was a thriving black market for any items related to the Beatles. It also helped influence the eventual tearing down of political walls as more oppressed people came to understand the value of having freedom of choice. Yeah, yeah, yeah!

An estimated seventy-three million viewers watched The Beatles first appearance on *The Ed Sullivan Show*. To this day it still stands as one of the highest-rated non-sports broadcasts of all time and almost forty years later was named "Rock'n Roll's Biggest TV Moment" by VH-1 and *Entertainment Weekly Magazine*. Adding to the legend was a report that no crimes were committed in New York City between 8 and 9 p.m. that Sunday night. It's also safe to say not much homework was done by the millions of young students who sat mesmerized over what was happening on their television screens.

I Me Mine

(For future references – because I know you'll be wondering – "I Me Mine" segments are my personal memories. Other contributors will be given proper billing, as you will see…).

I was ten years old the night both New York City crime and homework were put on hold for The Beatles. The only knowledge I had of The Fab Four was from a brief performance clip of *She Loves You*, aired on late night television's, *The Jack Parr Show*, on January 3, 1964. Though I've viewed it on video since, my first impression had been more visual than musical. Their hair was unlike anything I'd seen before on a man outside of history books and Moe from The Three Stooges. They also bounced along to the rhythmic beat of their songs on stage more

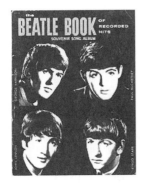

than the melancholy crooners of the early 1960's, who did a slick job of making pop music uninteresting to anyone under the age of eighteen.

I also remember Parr making jokes about the English group and their screaming fans. I didn't laugh or smile and it made me wonder why he'd poke fun at something a lot of kids seemed to enjoy. In hindsight, it was my first exposure to the never-ending generation gap. Whenever teenagers embrace something new, a segment of adult authority will always be ready to criticize what they are too old to understand.

During the next month, I had forgotten about The Beatles. Thanks to the above-mentioned melancholy crooners, I never listened to the radio. When I wasn't in school, playing with friends or doing homework, the best distraction was television. Among the hit programs of 1964 were *The Lucy Show, The Beverly Hillbillies, The Dick Van Dyke Show* and *The Flintstones.*

Fortunately, *The Ed Sullivan Show* was standard viewing in our household every Sunday night. Having just returned that evening from a weekend family vacation, I curled up on the floor with my back against the couch and watched The Beatles as they bounced into the song, *All My Loving.*

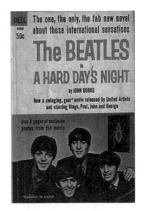

The effect on my young mind was similar to Dorothy being swept from Kansas and crash-landing in Oz. Not counting the image on our televisions screen, the world seemed to change from black and white to color, and I would never look at it the same way again.

DID YOU HEAR THE CHANGE?

I Me Mine

In the winter of 1966, I only had to wait until June to become a full-fledged teenager. It's tempting to say a "card-carrying member," but at the age of thirteen the only card I would be qualified for was one giving me the right to borrow books from the library.

Under the influence of the Beatles and the thriving pop music scene, boys were growing their hair longer, girls were wearing their skirts shorter - and both were noticing the other. In junior high school the newspaper headlines were discussed in Social Studies Class, while teen magazines were the source of information in our social circles. Since we were too young to vote or register for the military draft, our main concerns were music, fashion, and the opposite sex - not necessarily in that order.

The world had changed since The Beatles debut on *The Ed Sullivan Show*. The peaceful economic boom we had grown comfortable with was beginning to feel the rumblings of an undeclared war in Vietnam. The first demonstrations against the conflict occurred in March, but the escalation of soldiers and weapons continued. By April, President Lyndon B. Johnson was Commander In Chief of over 250,000 U.S. troops stationed in the small Asian country.

The Civil Rights Movement and efforts in the southern states to end discriminating tactics of race segregation led by The Reverend Martin Luther King were making headlines. His belief in peaceful protests were sometimes countered by violent resistance from white supremacists and anger simmered nationwide until the heat of summer erupted into full-scale riots in Cleveland, Detroit, Chicago, Los Angeles and other cities.

Astronauts were rocket jockeys in a space race to keep the moon free from Communism. China declared the Cultural Revolution to eliminate all political opponents of Chairman Mao and detonated a Hydrogen Bomb in May. The U.S. lost one of its own nuclear H-Bomb nightmares in the sea off the coast of Spain after a mid-air collision by two military aircraft. Russian leader Leonid Brezhnev demanded the U.S. withdraw from Vietnam, Fidel Castro declared martial law in Cuba citing fears the U.S. would attack, and our government launched its first stealth-designed spy plane to keep an eye in the sky over these growing international concerns.

The political world seemed to be in the throes of uncontrollable rage and aggression. Governments and organizations argued over control of territories, while minorities and the self-righteous fought injustice. Sides were taken and opinions were voiced. The Black Panther Party was formed, both foreign and home grown conspiracies were rumored to have assassinated President John F. Kennedy, and the radical youth vowed never to trust anyone over the age of thirty.

In terms of music, 1966 stands the test of time as an important crossroads between pop and rock. The three-chord guitar innocence and vocal harmony that grabbed the hearts and souls of young listeners only two years earlier had developed a rougher edge that would soon blossom into psychedelic, power pop, and heavy metal.

The generation of the 1960's lived from one hit record to the next with the "grooviest" dances and parties playing the "hippest" songs. There was no concept of Classic Rock or Oldies Radio, which decades later would be our only salvation from the future shock of urban rap and hip-hop music embraced by our own teenagers. Of

course this would give us a chance to continue the never-ending generation gap by criticizing something we didn't understand. But in 1966 our music was the current and evolving style that spoke youthful thoughts and opinions.

Songs of love, devotion and heartbreak have been themes since the beginnings of rock'n roll and will never go out of style. The attitudes and morals of Elvis Presley, Little Richard and Chuck Berry that shocked parents in the 1950's have been pushed further with each ensuing generation, keeping it meaningful, personal and rebellious for young listeners.

By 1966, the more creative pop musicians were now *artists* who had opinions to express about what was happening in the world. They wrote about different subjects or made their thoughts about love, devotion and heartbreak more personal than the songs of their predecessors. Song writers could get *high* from love, protest the war, or complain about injustice by making their messages heard through complex and abstract lyrics. Bob Dylan, Joan Baez and Pete Seeger had already expressed these themes in folk music, but it gained a much larger audience through pop. Experimental sounds from innovative studio techniques and the use of exotic instruments such as sitars, strings, horns and electronic keyboards combined with a back beat carried the weighty image of relevance that spoke to a generation through new record releases.

Some of the more popular groups from only a year earlier couldn't keep up with progressive musical scene. Gerry and The Pacemakers broke up and The Dave Clark Five were on their way out. Herman's Hermits became the teeny-bopper poster group, picking up the absence of a new Beatles film that year with the theatrical release of *Hold On!* At the same time, The Grateful Dead, Big Brother and the Holding Company, and Buffalo Springfield were playing their earliest shows in California.

The first sign of experimental music in the pop market came in late 1964 with John Lennon's guitar feedback at the beginning of *I Feel Fine.* The next year saw The Kinks - *You Really Got Me* - and

Rolling Stones - *(I Can't Get No) Satisfaction* - featuring a "fuzz" guitar as the main instrument. One of Paul McCartney's contributions to the B-side of The Beatles *Help!* soundtrack album was *Yesterday*, with the only instrumentation provided by a lone acoustic guitar and classical string quartet. The ballad has gone on to become the most covered song in history with over 3,000 recorded versions and helped pave the way for pop music to include orchestral arrangements.

The Beatles album *Rubber Soul* was still topping the charts and inspired Brian Wilson of The Beach Boys to create his masterpiece, *Pet Sounds*, released in May. When *Revolver* followed in August, Bob Dylan's earlier protest claim that *The Times They Are A'Changin'* took on a different meaning as a new musical wave swelled over 1966.

With the Beatles leading the way it would flood the market in 1967 with *Sgt. Pepper's Lonely Hearts Club Band* and open the gates for Jimi Hendrix, The Jefferson Airplane, Cream and others. The color of Oz was in the process of turning psychedelic.

Top Record Releases Of 1966

Singles:

The Beatles - *Day Tripper* / *We Can Work It Out* / *Nowhere Man* /
  Paperback Writer / *Rain* / *Yellow Submarine* / *Eleanor Rigby*
The Beach Boys - *Good Vibrations* / *Wouldn't It Be Nice* /
  Barbara Ann
Rolling Stones - *Paint It Black* / *19th Nervous Breakdown*
Young Rascals - *Good Lovin'*
Lovin' Spoonful – *Summer In The City*
Bobby Hebb – *Sunny*
The Supremes – *You Keep Me Hanging On* / *My World Is Empty*
  Without You
Percy Sledge - *When A Man Loves A Woman*
Sgt. Barry Sadler – *The Ballad of the Green Berets*
Righteous Brothers – *Soul And Inspiration*
The Association – *Cherish*
The Capitols - *Cool Jerk*
Four Tops – *Reach Out And I'll Be There*
The Mamas and The Papas - *California Dreamin'* / *Monday Monday*
The Troggs - *Wild Thing*
Tommy James & The Shondells – *Hanky Panky*
Donovan – *Mellow Yellow*
J.J. Jackson – *But It's Alright*
Surfaris – *Wipe Out*
Bob Dylan – *Rainy Day Women #12 & #35*
The Temptations – *Get Ready*
? and The Mysterians – *96 Tears*
Bobby Fuller Four – *I Fought The Law*
Lou Christie – *Lightening Strikes*
Paul Revere & The Raiders – *Hungry*
The Chiffons – *Sweet Talkin' Guy*

Crispin St. Peters – *The Pied Piper*
Tommy Roe – *Sweet Pea*
Los Bravos – *Black Is Black*
The Turtles – *You Baby*
The Happenings - *See You In September*
Four Seasons – *Working My Way Back To You*
Wilson Pickett – *Mustang Sally / Land of 1,000 Dances*
Herman's Hermits - *Leaning On A Lamp Post / This Door Swings Both Ways*
Ray Charles - *Cryin' Time*
The Byrds – *Eight Miles High*
Gary Lewis & The Playboys - *Sure Gonna Miss Her / Green Grass*
The Outsiders - *Time Won't Let Me*
The Who - *Happy Jack*
The Monkees - *Last Train To Clarksville / I'm A Believer*

Albums:

The Beatles - *Yesterday …and Today / Revolver*
The Beach Boys - *Pet Sounds*
Bob Dylan - *Blonde On Blonde*
The Byrds – *Fifth Dimension*
Simon & Garfunkel – *Sounds of Silence / Parsley, Sage, Rosemary and Thyme*
Rolling Stones – *Aftermath*
Cream – *Fresh Cream*
Frank Zappa – *Freak Out!*
Buffalo Springfield – *Buffalo Springfield*
Otis Redding – *Dictionary of Soul*
Jefferson Airplane – *Takes Off*
The Yardbirds – *Roger The Engineer*
John Mayall – *Bluesbreakers with Eric Clapton*
The Kinks – *Face To Face*

I READ THE NEWS TODAY – OH BOY!

With the Cold War, Civil Rights, the space race and the U.S. involvement in Vietnam, it wasn't often the daily lives of pop stars made newsworthy headlines in 1966. Relegated to the entertainment sections, gossip pages, or to give smiling news anchors an excuse to shake their heads in disbelief at the end of television news broadcasts, the stories were mostly about dealing with fame, screaming fans, hit records, tours, or other events that were far from ordinary. Established mainstream magazines and newspapers might run an article on a major pop artist to give the publication a youthful appeal - or warn parents that their children's idols were strictly entertainers and not role models.

Immediately following their debut in America, The Beatles were a major news story. During the week of April 4, 1964, they held the top five positions on the *Billboard Singles Chart* with *Can't Buy Me Love, Twist and Shout, She Loves You, I Want To Hold Your Hand* and *Please Please Me.*

The next week saw fourteen of their songs in the Top 100, breaking the record of nine held by Elvis Presley. *A Hard Day's Night* won surprising critical reviews and their appearances caused riots wherever they went.

The sheer magnitude of their fame deserved media coverage, but the novelty angle of "just being Beatles" had run its course over the years. What was once considered extraordinary was now expected. The Fab Four could still grab headlines, but each achievement had to be bigger than the one before.

On June 12, 1965, they were awarded the MBE, (Member of the Order of the British Empire), by Queen Elizabeth, igniting a controversy with war veterans who felt the group wasn't deserving of the honor. Later that summer, *Help!* was released and all attendance records for a pop concert were shattered when they kicked-off their American tour with a performance at New York's Shea Stadium.

For many dedicated fans, everything The Beatles did was a newsworthy event. Keeping track of their movements and thoughts, (both real and assumed), was the job of assorted teen magazines. Among the most popular were *Sixteen, Tiger Beat, Teen Screen,* and one that would later prove to be the most influential of all during their final concert tour - *Datebook*.

Mostly considered "fluff" with "kissable" photos, these magazines competed for exclusive inside information and gossip not only about The Beatles, but also other pop acts. Among those featured in any given issue would be Paul Revere & The Raiders, Peter and Gordon, Herman's Hermits, and the female stars of the day, Dusty Springfield, Cilla Black, and Petula Clark. Headlines promising what the stars liked, disliked and desired served as teasers on the covers, while the articles inside usually confirmed their basic public relations image as being wholesome for the entire family, with a general wish to make their fans happy. Controversial topics such as drugs, alcohol and sex were never reported. This could be attributed to the young age of the average reader - and to win parental approval when their teenager needed money to pay for the latest issue.

Coverage of The Beatles still dominated teen magazines in early 1966. With two movies suitable for the entire family and a blanket endorsement as "well-behaved youngsters" from Ed Sullivan himself, the group was considered safe for the general public.

In terms of popularity, The Beatles seemed to be an unstoppable force. Their 1965 Christmas release, *Rubber Soul*, still topped the album charts and the two-sided hit, *Day Tripper / We Can Work It Out*, was followed by *Nowhere Man*.

Then, out of nowhere, The Nowhere Man himself threw a Spaniard, (British slang for a monkey wrench), in the works with an interview printed in London's *The Evening Standard* newspaper, which included a quote that would haunt him for the rest of his life...

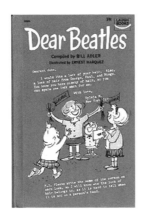

HOW DOES A BEATLE LIVE?

On March 4, 1966, *The Evening Standard* published an interview with John Lennon by journalist Maureen Cleave. Basically meant to be an article on the lifestyle of the chief Beatle, they had spent a day in his mansion talking about various topics including books and fame. When the subject turned to religion, his remarks caused a bigger reaction than either could have ever imagined.

In England, where the Beatles were considered national treasures as a money-making machine, Lennon's comments were hardly noticed within the long, rambling interview. To the British, he was a talented pop star with an artistic flair for being out-spoken in an entertaining, sarcastic and humorous way. If you believed the characterizations of each Beatle in their movies, *A Hard Day's Night* and *Help!* Lennon had a reputation for being "cheeky." In his homeland, this interview was only another example.

When The Beatles first landed in North America, their press conferences were as light-hearted as the songs *Love Me Do* and *I Want To Hold Your Hand*. Reporters, (most of whom probably couldn't tell one Beatle from the other), were given suggested questions and the group had practiced answers:

Q: "How did you find America?"
A: "Turn left at Greenland."
Q: "Will you sing for us?"
A: "We need money first."

Q: "Are you going to get a haircut?"
A: "I had one yesterday."

By 1966, The Beatles and their music had matured. The individual personalities displayed in their movies, (John the cynic; Paul as cute; George the quiet one; Ringo as a lovable pal), were the stereotypes both fans and media embraced. But as their success continued, so did opportunities to express their growing opinions about what was really happening in the world.

Many of their latest songs were about more personal and different topics than boy meets girl or boy loses girl. The lyrics could mask the true message for teenage consumption and catchy tunes still had everyone singing along - even if they didn't know what the composer of the song was actually writing about.

John in particular had a talent for wordplay that could hide a lyric's true meaning. He later claimed his jaunty title song for their film *Help!* was originally a slower ballad about his personal cry for help within the strict confines of being a Beatle. *Norwegian Wood* was actually about an affair he'd had while still married to his first wife, and *He Said She Said* came from an LSD trip in Los Angeles, when the actor Peter Fonda kept repeating to him, "I know what it's like to be dead."

Of course these revelations were never reported in teen magazines or on the evening news in 1966. The Beatles' public image was still carefully controlled by their manager Brian Epstein and press agent Tony Barrow. A wholesome image sold records and tickets, so The Fab Four continued to smile and wave in public.

Behind closed doors was a different story. The Beatles also had private lives in which they could let their hair down in front of family and certain friends. Among this inner group was a British journalist named Maureen Cleave.

The article, titled *How Does A Beatle Live? John Lennon Lives Like This*, was published in *The Evening Standard* on March 4, 1966. Basically, it's Cleave's report on what it was like to spend one day with "probably the laziest person in England – he can sleep almost indefinitely."

She describes the home he shared with his first wife Cynthia and their then three-year old son, Julian. A mock Tudor mansion in the upscale neighborhood of Weybridge, it was an area that normally attracted stockbrokers and bankers. The only exceptions seemed to be the Lennons – and the other two married Beatles, George and Ringo. They would drive to visit each other since "outdoors is for holidays." Paul was the only Beatle who still lived in London.

Lennon's house was filled with toys and gadgets that never seemed to work correctly, or that he grew tired of very quickly. Five televisions played constantly, along with records on various stereo systems. His latest passion was Indian music that George had "turned him onto." A suit of armor, (named Sidney), a room full of model cars, and Christmas presents he had never gotten around to giving out just collected dust. The presents were actually boxes of blinking red lights that were guaranteed to work until the next Christmas. They sat piled up in one room – blinking – but it was beginning to look like the guarantee wouldn't last the full twelve months.

In popularity, The Beatles were compared to The Queen. Their unprecedented worldwide fame as pop stars caused people to point and say, "It's the Queen" or "It's The Beatles," whenever a Rolls Royce with black windows passed on the street. It was also mentioned that "they share the security of a stable life at the top" as Her Royal Highness.

There were a number of quotes in the article that could have been controversial if taken out of context – had they not been overpowered by his remarks on religion. One concerned his thoughts about ugly people:

I couldn't stand ugly people even when I was five. Lots of the ugly ones are foreign, aren't they?

Another was his "morbid horror" of stupid people:

Famous and loaded as I am, I still have to meet soft people.

But the quote that would wash ashore in America on the eve of the Beatles' summer tour caused enough headlines to catch the attention of even "the laziest person in England." As the conversation turned to religion, Lennon told Cleave…

Christianity will go. It will vanish and shrink. I needn't argue about that; I'm right and I will be proved right. We're more popular than Jesus now. I don't know which will go first, rock'n roll or Christianity. Jesus was all right, but his disciples were thick and ordinary. It's them twisting it that ruins it for me.

Excerpts from: *How Does A Beatle Live? John Lennon Lives Like This*
By Maureen Cleave

ALBUMS, SINGLES & THE BUTCHER COVER

The wheels were already in motion during the spring of 1966 for another Beatles summer tour. Shows in Germany would be their first in the country since they were a struggling group on the Hamburg music scene, while visits to Japan and The Philippines were seen as a continuation of the group's worldwide conquest. Touring America had become an annual event and with the planned addition of more outdoor stadium shows, it was expected to be bigger than any before.

In hindsight, an argument could be made that the German concerts in late June of 1966 marked the end of Beatlemania as a highly-anticipated and well-received traveling road show. As a group they would never again be able to perform in a foreign country without threat of demonstrations, violence, injury and even possible death. What followed during the remaining months of summer was enough of a nightmare to stop them from ever touring together again - even without the coming reaction in The United States over Lennon's remarks concerning The Beatles being more popular than Jesus.

Rubber Soul was just ending its reign topping international music charts when John, Paul, George and Ringo gathered at the Oluf Nissen Photographic Studio on March 25th, where Robert Whitaker took the official photos used in the 1966 tour program and promotional hand-outs for the media. During this session, The Beatles also posed for the notorious *Butcher Cover* originally used on the American album *Yesterday and Today*.

In a playful mood and anxious for something more artistic than just standing and smiling for the camera, The Beatles improvised off the photographer's suggestions. Dressed in dark turtleneck sweaters, they were draped in yards of colorful fabrics, posed in front of a reflective background and even laid on the floor in a circle with their four mop-tops together. When Whitaker produced heads, limbs and torsos of plastic baby dolls, along with butcher smocks and raw meat, the first dent in the Beatles seemingly invincible armor of popularity was about to take a direct hit.

Until *Sgt. Pepper's Lonely Hearts Club Band* was released the following year, Beatle albums in The United States varied from those in England and other parts of the world. Executives at Capitol Records, their American distributor, were convinced that hit singles sold albums and songs such as *I Want To Hold Your Hand, She Loves You, I Feel Fine* and *Day Tripper* had to be included. On the other hand, the Beatles and their English record company EMI, kept to a policy that fans shouldn't have to pay for the same songs twice and didn't use hit singles on albums.

Capitol also included fewer songs, which resulted in more albums for the American market. The U.S. versions of *A Hard Day's Night* and *Help!* included instrumental soundtrack music, even though the Beatles had recorded songs for these albums that did not appear in either film. The backlog was issued in *Something New* and *Beatles VI,* which were never released in England. Other variations include *Meet The Beatles, The Beatles Second Album, The Early Beatles, Beatles '65* and *Hey Jude.*

Yesterday and Today, scheduled for release in June, followed this practice. It included the hit singles *Day Tripper, We Can Work It Out, Nowhere Man* and *Yesterday*, along with the B-sides, *What Goes On* and *Act Naturally.*

If I Needed Someone, Drive My Car and *I'm Only Sleeping* were originally intended for *Rubber Soul. And Your Bird Can Sing* and *Doctor Robert* were lifted from the upcoming *Revolver,* which would once again have fewer songs than its English counterpart when released in August.

The summer of 1966 was already simmering under a forecast of heat, protest and violence. For fans looking at the coming Beatles tour as a cool breeze of diversion from the growing stress in the world, those dreams were about to crack under pressure. *The Butcher Cover* and Lennon's quotes were poised to make headlines and the backlash waiting for them in North America would be unprecedented for a pop music group.

But at least city officials in Cleveland wouldn't have to worry about the uproar surrounding a visit by The Beatles. They had been banned from the city since their 1964 concert at Public Hall.

BANNED IN CLEVELAND
September 15, 1964

Practically unknown in The United States only seven months earlier, The Beatles' 1964 summer tour was unlike anything this country had seen since Elvis first shook his hips under a mountain of greasy hair. Hot on the success of *A Hard Day's Night*, released on August 11th, a visit by The Fab Four could almost paralyze a city. Mobs of fans surrounded hotels, stopped traffic and screamed loud enough to inspire serious journalists to write articles questioning the sanity of this younger generation. Their concerts were opportunities for teenagers to loudly worship their idols in person, while local police assigned to protect the group viewed these events as potential riots.

For almost a month, beginning in San Francisco on Wednesday, August 19th, the group performed in twenty-five cities throughout North America. Astute concert promoters and radio stations knew The Beatles would be a hot ticket and money-making venture, and Tuesday, September 15th was secured for a performance at Public Hall in downtown Cleveland. Radio station WHK-AM was chosen to sponsor the event, but it took a creative effort by three dedicated sales people to make it happen.

In 1964, Norman Wain was an account executive at WHK. He had started his radio career in the early 1950's as a deejay, (Big Chief Norman), and later formed the Westchester Corporation with partners Bob Weiss and Joe Zingale. The company owned and operated AM and FM radio stations in major metropolitan markets including Cleveland, Washington DC, St. Louis, Orlando, Tampa, Charlotte and others. As owner and CEO, he was also instrumental in building and operating WOIO Television Channel 19 in Cleveland.

Norman Wain

Bob Weiss, Joseph Zingale and I were the local sales staff for WHK. We found out the Beatles were not going to come to Cleveland during their first North American tour and we thought that was terrible. We also decided that would be a great promotion for WHK. You know, we were the sales people and obviously anything that helped the station helped us sell time.

But we weren't able to get in touch with our management. Jack Thayer, our manager, was out of town making a speech or something, so the three of us conspired to get the Beatles to Cleveland one way or the other.

Our big rival at the time was KYW, which was the big 50,000 watt rocker. So we found out what booking agency was bringing them in and it turned out to be The Music Corporation of America, (MCA). We called them and said, "What can we do to make you bring the Beatles to Cleveland on their North American tour? You can't snub Cleveland."

They said, "Well, first of all, one of the reasons we're not coming is that there's no venue for them. And anyway, we want to deal with KYW." And KYW was hotly pursuing it because the idea was that any station that had them would have a tremendous public relations coup.

What we did was this. We sent Joe Zingale to New York and he sat with the MCA people. He called us and said, "Listen, you gotta send me a telegram from Public Hall. They're willing to come to Cleveland, but only if there's a hall or someplace for them to perform."

Bob and I went down to Public Hall and met with the manager. He said the hall was open that date and he'd give it to anybody who wants to bring the Beatles in. So we said to him, "How about us?"

He said, "Well, I'm not so sure. KYW is better and they're bigger. You guys are only in sales and you're not even the management. I'm not sure we're going to do that."

So anyway, we went back to the station and sent Joe a fake telegram saying, "Dear Joe, we just locked up Public Hall for the September 15th date." Then we went back to Public Hall, and we told the manager that we've got the Beatles all locked-up. So we told two lies and the Beatles said they would come in with WHK. We beat out KYW. It was wild.

We had contests to give-away tickets and built the hysteria as much as we could. There were articles in *The Plain Dealer* and we did everything possible to make it a big and exciting event.

Harry Martin was a popular deejay in San Diego when Westinghouse Radio, owner of the 50,000 watt giant KYW, persuaded him to team with Specs Howard for a morning show in Cleveland. With WHK securing the Beatles concert at Public Hall, they were moving into position to win the ratings war. Martin and Howard's job was to preserve their station's dominance and keep KYW number one with listeners.

The duo's infectious on-air humor wrapped around the top hits of the day earned "The Martin and Howard Show" the coveted top position until they moved on to Detroit in 1967. Both have been inducted into The Radio Television Broadcasters Hall of Fame of Ohio and enjoyed success in other major markets. But in Cleveland, they still have the infamous reputation as being the ones who "scooped" WHK and saved the Beatles concert.

Harry Martin

It shows you that being mischievous doesn't pay. WHK committed a venial sin. It was serendipity and silliness that got it back for KYW. There was never any formality of KYW presenting it, but I've had people tell me they were always under the impression that it was a "KYW Presents" concert, mainly because we got on stage. Specs and I decided to grab a couple of tickets and check out our reputedly unbeatable adversaries at WHK and of course, to catch the Fab Four. Then that night we just fell into it and stole the Beatle concert from WHK.

WHK continued to build excitement for weeks over the show. Requests for tickets had been so overwhelming that a mail-in lottery system was used to determine who would be lucky enough to attend. By the time The Beatles landed in Cleveland on September 14th, following a concert that same night in Pittsburgh, fans and press were waiting at Hopkins Airport. John, Paul, George and Ringo jumped into a limousine that took them downtown to The Sheraton Cleveland Hotel and their quarters in the Governor's Suite.

The Beatles settled in, knowing the next day would be a continuation of the tour routine they had become used to. There would be a press conference for the Cleveland media, where they were expected to give witty answers to questions they had already been asked in other cities throughout the tour, followed by a brief "meet and greet" with lucky contest winners from WHK. That evening they would perform their concert at Public Hall and then fly to New Orleans to do it all again the next day.

In 1964, Ron Sweed was only fourteen years old, but already working for one of the most popular characters in the history of Cleveland television: Ghoulardi. Portrayed by television and radio veteran, Ernie Anderson, who later went on to a Hollywood career as announcer for *The Carol Burnett Show, America's Funniest Home Videos* and many others, Ghoulardi was the host of *Shock Theater*, broadcast live every Friday at 11:20 p.m. on Channel 8, following *City Camera News*.

The character of Ghoulardi was a mix of cool beatnik and mad scientist, with a Bela Lugosi vampire accent. Costumed in a fake mustache and goatee, fright wig, and sunglasses with only one lens, it didn't matter what low-grade, B-movie was featured each night. Teenage fans would tune in to watch his outrageous antics during commercial breaks, when he would use firecrackers to blow-up plastic models, toys, or anything else he could think of, while insulting other local personalities of the day. It was pure anti-establishment hi-jinks and as his popularity continued to grow with baby-boomers, Channel 8 added a Saturday afternoon version of the show. Thirty years later, Cleveland native Drew Carey would display his lasting devotion by wearing a faded Ghoulardi T-shirt in many episodes of *The Drew Carey Show*.

Sweed's position, gloriously described as "gofer" in the book, *Ghoulardi: Inside Cleveland TV's Wildest Ride* by Tom Feren and R.D. Heldenfels, was an apprenticeship that would eventually lead to his own television and radio fame. When Anderson left for California, Sweed filled the broadcast void as an off-shoot character named The Ghoul, and has enjoyed a career spanning almost four decades with his show syndicated in numerous markets throughout the country.

As the resident teenager in 1964, Sweed was also Anderson's pipeline of information about of what was "cool" and "hip" with the boomers who made up the majority of Ghoulardi's viewers. Sweed's enthusiasm and association with both the show and Channel 8 eventually led to several memorable encounters with the Beatles.

Ron Sweed

I was all around the station. I knew all the photographers, the news guys, the weather guys, and all the office staff. It was like one big family. It was just a magical time.

Everybody knew I was crazy about the Beatles and I would bring the current Beatle music for Ghoulardi's show. I brought my Paul McCartney Beatle Bubble Bath and Ringo Starr Beatle Bubble Bath down to the station and Ghoulardi blew them up on the air. I feel bad about it now, especially when I see those prices people would pay for it today.

I painstakingly painted the Revel Ringo Starr model kit and - BAM! - it was blown to smithereens on Ghoulardi's show. In the background would be "She loves you yeah, yeah, yeah!" I brought that record in for his Saturday afternoon show. He had been out at all the stores downtown trying to find a copy, but it was sold-out everywhere. So when he came in and saw it he went, "Hey Ron, you got it! Great!"

In 1964 the press guys knew how much it would mean to me to meet the Beatles. So they shared their press passes with me and I was able to go to the press conference at the Sheraton Hotel. That was the first year I got to meet them and shake their hands.

Then it was just craziness when you walked out of that hotel. Everybody that knew you were in there or had anything to do with the Beatles treated you like royalty. At the Sheraton there was a little café and they were like, "Oh, you're with the Beatles? Here, you don't have to pay for anything. What do you want to eat? What do you want to drink?" You know, that sort of thing.

I was also able to go to the concert. Ernie Anderson had two tickets. He gave me one of them and gave his son the other.

Norman Wain

We sat and talked with the Beatles for a long time at the hotel while girls were screaming and trying to wave at them from the street. As a matter of fact, one girl actually hid in a dumb waiter. She hid under the linens and when it came to the eighth floor she jumped out and ran into the room trying to get to the Beatles. That's how crazy the kids were.

I got to know them a little bit and I saw that John and Paul were really the heart and soul of the group. And the guys were just so unassuming and plain. They had no idea they were rewriting music history. They had no idea they were becoming a worldwide phenomenon. They really felt they were still back in Liverpool and they were a band of four guys playing the music they liked.

They were very much influenced, they told me, by American rock and roll. Fats Domino was one of their big heroes. They loved all the sounds that came out of the black and country experience and it all shaped their music. But at the same time they felt they were doing something uniquely their own.

Ron Sweed

John Lennon was my favorite. He had been so before I met him and it stayed the same after I met him. I always said he and Ernie Anderson could've been father and son because they both had this sharp sense of humor. It was a razor sharp wit. And both John Lennon and Ernie Anderson disliked people that had attitudes and took themselves too seriously.

I saw John Lennon use his several times, because they had their share of pompous news people that tried to act like the Beatles were insignificant and these newsmen were the all important people. John would just chew them up and spit them out in no time – in the twinkling of an eye. And he would do it in such a way that the poor idiot didn't even realize it, but everyone around him would be laughing at this guy because John had just totally made a fool of him.

One instance was Joel Daily, who was doing *City Camera News* at the time. Joel was pretty taken with himself and one of his questions at the press conference was: "Mr. Lennon. What do you think about all these psychiatrists who psychoanalyze your fans about how they scream and you can't even hear yourselves and your singing. What's your approach to their analyzation of all these people?"

John looked out at him and said, "Well, they have nothing better to do. Do they? These psychiatrist types…"

Everybody started laughing. And Daily just looks around, sits back down and shuts up.

Following the press conference, the Beatles were escorted the few blocks through downtown Cleveland to Public Hall for their 8 p.m. concert. The opening acts were The Bill Black Combo, The Exciters, The Righteous Brothers and Jackie DeShannon. Then, greeted by the deafening sound of 10,000 screaming fans, the Beatles were introduced and performed their first three songs, *Twist and Shout, You Can't Do That* and *All My Loving,* before the audience was overwhelmed by the excitement.

Ron Sweed

I remember the reports always said, "You can't hear them." At the concerts I went to, I always heard them fine. That was one of my first memories from the '64 show, besides seeing them live on stage and how cool that was.

But the screaming, I mean no doubt about it – it was there! It was like a siren for the whole half hour going, "Errr! Errr! Errr!" It felt like it was an audio blanket.

The flashbulbs going off were like a video blanket, because that was the mode of photography at the time. They always used those Kodak flashbulbs that would pop out and the floor would be covered with them. And when they went off, all flashing at once, it was like a sheet of lightening. So besides that audio blanket that I liken to a siren at the time, it was like a lightening storm, because it was non-stop from start to finish. Amid all of that going on, what I remember - and I must have heard it quite well – was that, "Boy they sound great!"

Norman Wain

There were only 10,000 seats and we could've sold 20,000 tickets. The problem was that the police really weren't expert at controlling crowds. It was one of the first for a rock group that big in that arena. The police were standing at the stage and instead of looking at the audience; they were looking at the Beatles. So there were all kinds of raucousness and riots.

The fans had turned the scene into a mad rush for the stage. Young girls and boys jumped from their seats and ran down the aisles, screaming for the group. Some grabbed at the microphone stands, almost pulling them into the audience, while others threw themselves onto the stage as the Beatles continued to play.

Harry Martin

When Specs Howard and I got there, all hell was breaking loose. We were deafened by the shrill screams of 10,000 young girls driven

over the edge just by the idea of being in the same place as their beloved Beatles. They were just screaming and raising hell and crashing through the police cordon. I've always had the feeling that a dozen dedicated fourteen year old girls could break through the defensive line of the Cleveland Browns if they wanted to. They were also mauling the WHK jocks - who panicked and ran out the stage door.

Public Hall was in a state of pandemonium as more kids ran down from the upper seating levels and pushed their way past police and to the stage. In an email sent to **beatlesincleveland.com**, one fan describes the scene from his perspective in the audience.

John T.

I will never, ever forget the thrill of that event. I managed to sneak along the outside lobby corridors and slip into the first group of doors leading to rows one through ten and jumped on a vacated chair, probably belonging to some girl who had rushed closer to the stage. I clearly remember the thrill of the moment as the Beatles were THERE, playing no further than maybe twenty-five feet in front of me. Tell me I wasn't a kid who thought he was the luckiest in the world at that moment. From row twenty-two to the first row?!

This was at a part of the show when everything was getting out of control and people were storming the stage, going completely nuts.

And a police officer actually held my legs as I stood on a chair so I wouldn't fall. I kept thinking to myself, "Man, nobody is gonna believe this!"

Norman Wain

And at one point the Police Commissioner or I guess the Chief of Police, walked on stage and said, "Unless everybody sits down, we're going to stop the concert."

Harry Martin

We happened to be walking past the police chief when he said, "Get them out of here! This concert is CLOSED!" This was one of those "eureka" moments. I knew the show was cancelled, or that he was going to cancel it. I forget just who it was, Specs or me who got the idea, but we ran to the chief and hollered into his ear, "Don't do that! Give us a chance to calm them down."

He didn't know us at all and didn't know that it's a cutthroat business with jocks out to get each other or any of that type of thing. But we introduced ourselves and he knew KYW, which was a big institution in Cleveland before it rocked. It was a big NBC station and he saw us as just two guys, which is basically true, that wanted to save the concert. So he said to go ahead and take a shot.

We'd had a lot of experience with screaming out of control teenagers, but frankly, our first instinct was for humanitarian reasons. We knew it was a WHK concert, but the kids were there to see the Beatles. Honest to goodness we knew how disappointed these little girls were going to be, because this guy was going to cancel it. So we said let's see what we can do.

There was no sign of the WHK guys. They were hiding backstage. So I told the chief to make sure the WHK guys don't come up on stage because the crowd will see them and go crazy again. So one way or another, we never saw them when we went up there. We simply walked through all the cops who were still standing guard and went to the stage.

John T

I distinctly remember Lennon arguing with the Fire Marshall onstage not to stop the show. Here I am, thirteen years old and watching all this go down from my first row perch. Rows and rows of seat back bleacher seats had fallen over like rows of dominoes from people standing, not on the seats, but on the chair backs to see. If I remember correctly, fans had even brought tied up sheets and, acting much like a prison break from a third story cell, they were trying to climb down it from the balcony and onto the stage.

Insanity reigned everywhere with everyone caught up in the moment; one they knew would be historical and remembered forever. They ended up delaying the show for twenty to thirty minutes until everyone could shake the hysteria that flowed and energized throughout the whole building.

From her balcony seat to the right of the stage, young fan Becky B. had a clear view of the wild scene happening just below her. She remembers in a message to **beatlesincleveland.com**:

Becky B.

The girls on the main floor got up on their chairs to get a better view. Then they were falling off the chairs and rushing the stage. They had to stop the show and put down the fire curtain. Someone came out and said if everyone would PLEASE sit down, they would allow the show to continue. They said the Fire Marshall could not allow the show to go on if people did not get away from the stage.

Harry Martin

We both ran to the center of the stage heedless of our lives and hollered into the microphone, "Hi there, we are Martin and Howard of KYW Radio." Specs announced, "We have just spoken to the chief and he wants to cancel the concert. Do you want this?"

"NO! NO!" everybody screamed. And they all became little girls again, instead of the monsters that they had been. We said, "We told the chief that Cleveland girls are the greatest girls in the world and all we have to do is just count to three and by the time we get to three, you'll be back in your seats."

And sure enough, we very slowly counted to three. "ONE…" and you could hear this rumbling of people running back to their chairs. "TWO… THREE!"

Becky B.

Amazingly, the crowd calmed down and returned to their seats. However, some of the folding chairs were broken or pushed away and it was impossible to return the main floor to order.

Harry Martin

I assure you, when Specs and I first went on our motivation, at least in the beginning, was to simply save the concert. Then as we got on stage, it was a little more calculating and we started plugging KYW unabashedly. We said, "Make sure you tune into KYW on Monday morning because we'll be playing THREE Beatle songs in a

ROW!" We managed to get our plug in. And exponential mathematics being what it is, the word got around from 10,000 little girls that said Martin and Howard of KYW saved the Beatles concert. And 10,000 told another 10,000 that told another 10,000 and so I think half of Afghanistan knew about it by the following Monday.

And timing being what it is, just when we got to, "Make sure you listen to KYW," the curtain roared opened and there they were! When we saw that, Specs and I hollered at the top of our lungs, "And here they are – The Beatles!" You know, we  were just reacting to the curtain and everybody was going crazy – again. They were playing and singing, "She loves you, yeah, yeah, yeah!" Only no one heard them over the screams. We ran off stage and the Beatles went on with their concert. The WHK guys never came back out. They were not around. To this day I have no idea where they were, but we were known as the saviors of the Beatles concert. We were the number one show in the next ratings book and never looked back.

Becky B.

Girls were fainting, throwing things and screaming. It was unbelievable. The screaming was so loud we couldn't hear much of anything. Perhaps a bit of Ringo's bass drum from time to time, but that was it. I borrowed some opera glasses from the girl next to me and was able to read their lips since I had memorized the lyrics to most of their songs. I also screamed once at the top of my lungs, just because everyone else was. I literally could not hear myself at all!

John T.

Then McCartney declared, "Now for our last song for the night!" before breaking into *Long Tall Sally* and causing complete and utter chaos. I could see John and George laughing about the cops, who were guarding the stage, getting stormed yet again. I've relived that moment a million times since with a satisfaction of knowing that for once, that night, I was in the right place at the right time.

Harry Martin

The Beatles had been in their dressing rooms when Specs and I went on stage and had been told that the concert was shut down. Years later I saw Paul McCartney on a cable television interview and he was talking about the Cleveland concert. He said they had been told it was cancelled because of the riot and they were getting ready to pack up and leave.

"Then a few minutes later," he said, "a cop came into our dressing room and told us that we could go on stage and play. I never did learn what happened, that they changed their minds." To this day, he still doesn't know.

That's the reason he thought the show was cancelled, because it had been. So if he reads this book, it'll be a revelation for Sir Paul.

There were repercussions for this outburst of youthful enthusiasm, which was considered unacceptable by community leaders. In an unexpected hit to the city budget, it had cost more than $14,000 to protect The Beatles from their fans while in Cleveland. Another concern was for the safety of these same fans while attending pop music concerts.

Celebrated rock music columnist, Jane Scott, who two decades later was instrumental in bringing The Rock and Roll Hall of Fame and Museum to Cleveland, was Teen Editor for the *Cleveland Plain Dealer Newspaper*. In a career that spanned almost thirty-five years, she covered every important rock concert in Cleveland and reported the onstage and backstage highlights to her loyal readers. She was a fixture on the rock'n roll scene well into her seventies and on a first name basis with most of the stars.

Jane Scott

Mayor Ralph Locher banned The Beatles from coming to Cleveland during their 1965 tour. At the 1964 show, the kids were standing up and yelling and screaming. He thought, "Gosh, that isn't the way little girls should be acting." They just walked down the aisles a little bit and they screamed a lot, but they couldn't help it. The Rolling Stones were already scheduled to come in later that year, but when the parents read about what Mayor Locher said, they thought it was much more dire than it really was. So the parents wouldn't take their kids to Public Hall. The young kids had no way to get to the show. The Rolling Stones lost $5,000 and Mayor Locher banned all pop music concerts.

Norman Wain

It was a new game and nobody really knew how to control crowds or do those types of things. That's what led to the ban.

Songs Performed by The Beatles on the 1964 North American Tour:

Twist And Shout
You Can't Do That
All My Loving
She Loves You
Things We Said Today
Roll Over Beethoven
Can't Buy Me Love
If I Fell
I Want To Hold Your Hand
Boys
A Hard Day's Night
Long Tall Sally

For some shows, The Beatles would open with…

I Saw Her Standing There

On those nights, they would close with…

Twist And Shout and not play…

She Loves You

A NEW WAVE

When the Beatles returned to North America in the summer of 1965, they were riding another wave of unprecedented success. Their second movie, *Help!* had fans screaming at their celluloid images, while the movie soundtrack album and title song were both sitting at the number one position on the music charts. Their next single, *Yesterday*, would soon be on its way to becoming the most recorded song in history.

The tour began with a performance at New York's Shea Stadium in front of 56,000 fans on August 15th. But nowhere on the schedule was a concert in Cleveland. The Beatles were still banned.

In 1965, Jerry G. was Cleveland radio's direct connection with the Beatles. After starting his career as Jerry Ghan at a small station near his hometown of Chicago, he was hired in 1963 by the Cleveland Top 40 station, KYW-AM, and was known simply as "Jerry G." for the next four years. After the Beatles hit North America in 1964, his nightly *Beatles Countdown* program made him one of the most-listened to deejays in the broadcast area. His popularity led to another nightly hit, *On The Beatle Beat*, and his own weekly television show, *The Jerry G. Show*, featuring appearances by the top pop groups touring through Cleveland. He later moved on to radio fame in Chicago as Jerry G. Bishop and portrayed the creepy late night host Svengoolie for the television show, *Screaming Yellow Theater*.

Jerry G. traveled with the Beatles during their 1965 and 1966 North American tours. Spending time with the group on airplanes, in hotels, backstage and at concerts, his listeners were kept riveted to their radios as he shared interviews and eyewitness accounts of Beatlemania for *On The Beatle Beat.*

Jerry G. Bishop

I was on KYW and then NBC changed it to WKYC. The station said, "Do you want to go on The Beatle tour?" Of course – who would say no?"

They didn't play Cleveland in 1965. Ralph Locher, the Mayor, had banned the shows because in 1964 they had to stop the concert. The police were on stage. They finished it, but the police freaked. You know, it was the early days of rock'n roll. Woodstock hadn't happened yet. They didn't know how to react to this type of thing. The fans got excited, that's what kids do, so they stopped the concert and didn't let them come back in '65.

I first met them in New York at the Shea Stadium concert. I was in the third base dugout. Nobody ever thought they'd sell-out Shea Stadium, but they ended up turning people away. It was amazing. And at that point, that's when it hit me. This is a big deal. This is no little rock'n roll band.

At the beginning, it was my job. The station said, "Go and travel with this band." I'd been playing Beatles songs and I knew how big they were on that level, as a guy on the radio talking to an audience. I did a show every night at nine o'clock for two years called *The Beatle Countdown.* Every night. We'd get three to four hundred postcards A DAY voting for their favorite song. Kids would tune in to hear what the number one Beatle song OF THE DAY was!

But I had no idea how big they really were until Shea Stadium. I realized this is more than rock'n roll. This is history, because sociologically, they made so many changes. The way they dressed, the way we dressed. The fact that men have long hair, I'm convinced, is because of the Beatles. I had it for a long time too. Now I'm just happy to have hair!

But that's just small things that they changed. They changed attitudes. They made rock'n roll much more acceptable. You have to remember that in 1964, there was still that Right Wing fundamentalist mentality, probably more in the south than anywhere else, that kids were ruining the morality. I heard all that the first day I played a rock'n roll record on the radio.

Ron Sweed

In 1965, because of the Beatle Ban by Mayor Locher, Channel 8 sent me to Toronto to meet a photographer at the Maple Leaf Garden. He shot the press conference and the concert, and I brought the pictures back with me so they could use them on *City Camera News*. That was my '65 Beatle encounter; one press conference and two concerts at Maple Leaf Garden. Again I got to talk with them, shake their hands and everything.

I remember the Toronto press conference because the Beatles were always being asked the most inane questions. There wasn't a question they hadn't heard, so they're answering the same stuff over and over again.

Some of the questions were valid, while others weren't. Like, "What shampoo do you use?" and "How many times a day do you wash your hair?"

It wasn't long after Ringo had gotten married to Maureen and a reporter asked him, "Ringo, how did you propose to your wife?" You could just see in Ringo's face that he's thinking what the hell kind of question is that?

He goes, "I don't know, I suppose, just like anyone else." And you just see his poor, perplexed face like, how would the reporter answer that? So he looks at the guy and he said, "Are you married?"

The reporter goes, "No, but when I do propose I want to do it right."

And Lennon just – BOOM – shoots back to him, "Use both hands." The whole place went crazy laughing. Those are my memories of them. They just had a killer sense of humor and didn't take themselves seriously. They took their music seriously, but all the craziness that was around them, it was just a big laugh.

Jerry G. Bishop

The first time I heard them it was like an explosion. The

flashbulbs were more impressive than the noise. I mean we've all heard noise. But the flash involves 55,000 thirteen-year old girls, all with these little instant cameras flashing like a strobe light - constantly. They just changed those little flash cubes and they were all over the field.

I was out in San Francisco at The Cow Palace in 1965. It was a big barn of an auditorium. And they had built a twenty-five foot high stage for the Beatles, because they realized early on that the kids would just be climbing up there. And their roadies, a couple of real big guys... One was Malcolm Evans, who was like six-foot-six. He was like a building and he would stand at the apron of the stage. The kids would stand on each other's shoulders – it was amazing – and if any got up on stage, Malcolm would just pick them up and throw them back in the crowd.

I can't describe the noise, but I'm standing next to the stage in San Francisco and there's a cop right next to me. He yells, "I've never seen anything like this!" You had to talk that way, loud and right in each other's ear to be heard.

We're ten feet away from the Beatles and their amps, and I said, "Yeah, isn't that something?!" Then I turned away to look up at the stage again.

When I turned back, he was gone. I looked down and he's on the floor bleeding from the head. Somebody had thrown a Coke bottle. Some kid. Remember the old Coca Cola bottles with those little hour glass shapes? It had hit him in the head. So I got another guy and we schlepped him backstage and got him to first aid. That's how scary it was.

The kids were throwing jelly beans. One of them, I think Paul, had made the mistake of saying they liked jelly beans. Well, that was the fans' way of contacting the Beatles. They couldn't touch a Beatle, but if they threw something that hit a Beatle, that would be like touching a Beatle.

In April 1966, Brian Epstein, announced an August tour of The U.S. and Canada that included 19 shows in 14 cities. And though it would be almost two years since fans disrupted their concert at

Public Hall, Cleveland would again be bypassed. The August 14th date was scheduled for Louisville, Kentucky.

Jerry G. Bishop

I don't know if a Beatles concert was good or bad for a city. I think it came and went. The kids who were there all remember it and it's a part of their lives. But I think for the municipalities themselves, it was probably a pain in the ass. They needed extra police, extra first aid guys, city services had to block off roads, the airport... So in that respect, it was probably more trouble than it was worth.

At the time, not even the Beatles realized it would be their final concert tour. They also didn't foresee the group would be riding on the news-worthy crest of a different type of wave: controversy.

In March, *The Evening Standard* ran the interview with John Lennon that included his quote, "The Beatles are more popular than Jesus." According to books and articles written since, the remark was hardly noticed in England. When it was reprinted in the American fan magazine *Datebook* in late July, it caused an uproar of life-threatening proportions aimed at Lennon.

During the ensuing years, many Beatle historians and fans assumed the Louisville show was rerouted to Cleveland because of protests and death threats surrounding their appearance in the central area of the U.S. known as The Bible Belt. In reality, the location was changed months before *Datebook* hit newsstands. The Beatles were too popular to be banned in Cleveland any longer, but the real reason behind the show being cancelled in Louisville is explained by one of the concert's original promoters.

Don Schwartz

Yes, Louisville had an August concert date and myself, Tim Tyler, and Martin Cohn were to be the joint promoters. We had a verbal agreement, but unfortunately the contract was never signed because we could not find a location for them to play. The Kentucky Fair and Exposition Center would not allow us to use any part of their facility because it conflicted with the Kentucky State Fair. We tried Churchchill Downs, looked into putting it on in a field south of Louisville and any other place big enough, but we could not come up with a venue. That is the true and simple story. The threats played no role in them not coming to Louisville.

Jerry G. Bishop

I wasn't aware of any fear on the part of the Beatles. I was on that tour and I wasn't aware that they cancelled any shows. Louisville must have been cancelled before the tour began, because I remember when we got the itinerary in 1966 and it was Cleveland. There was nothing about Louisville, so that's news to me.

Norman Wain

In 1965 we, (Wain, Weiss and Zingale), quit WHK, went to New York and bought a radio station in White Plains. A year later we came back to Cleveland as the new owners of WDOK-AM and FM. We changed the call letters on the AM station to WIXY 1260. We modeled it after WABC in New York and made it into the biggest promotional Top 40 station you can possibly imagine. It was just wild. People listened to the station not just for the music, but to know what was going on because we had so many contests and promotions and bringing in acts and everything else.

Among the original line-up of deejays on WIXY was Johnny Canton, who held down the "drive time" shift from 4 to 7 p.m. Later that year, after also serving as the station's Program Director, he moved to Minneapolis-St. Paul to continue his very successful career in radio. In the fall of 2006, he was inducted into the Minnesota Broadcasting Hall of Fame.

Johnny Canton

We were a fledging little radio station coming on board with rock'n roll in January of 1966 and going up against WHK and WKYC. Both were pretty accepted Top 40 radio stations, so we had nothing to do but try to make it. Booking the Beatles would be our way into the big boys lounge.

Norman Wain

Top 40 in those days was much broader. It really was the tops on each chart. We played the top country record, the top R&B record, the top pop record, the top everything. It's much better radio, by the way.

Johnny Canton:

When we first went Top 40, we didn't have any commercials. All we could do is play nothing but music. Of course that's what the listeners were looking for and we could supply them with music. Eventually we started getting some commercials to make money.

Norman Wain

There were two reasons we didn't have commercials. One, it was a brand new format and we didn't have time to sell it to anybody. But the second reason was that we decided to go commercial free for the first couple of weeks just to get people to tune in. It was a big promotion for us. The buzz started like crazy: "Hey – 1260 on the dial has no commercials. Tune them in!" You know.

Johnny Canton

When Norman Wain, Joe Zingale and Bob Weiss had an opportunity to book the Beatles, they were rather reticent to do it because of the cost. It was like $75,000. That doesn't seem like a lot of money now, but at that time it was. And it was all cash up front. Their manager, Brian Epstein… well, the group was hot and you make hay while the sun shines. So they had to cough up the money. They asked us if we thought it was worth it and everyone said yes. Of course it's worth it, so they did commit.

Norman Wain

In '66, the Beatles were planning another American tour. By that time, we knew already who the MCA people were, so we contacted them again. We said we're the same group of people, even though it's a different radio station and not WHK:

"We brought you to Cleveland in '64 and it was a big success for you then. We'd like for you to come in '66 at we'll get a bigger arena, because obviously, we could've sold double the number of tickets."

They said fine.

Honestly, I don't know how we got the ban lifted. I know we had good contacts at City Hall and that we went down there and spoke to them about it. But I think the fact that we were in the stadium made a big difference because the police liked the idea that it was out in the open and more easily controlled. I think that's what happened.

Johnny Canton

It makes sense that we got the concert because it defaulted in Louisville. I'm sure the promoters went around to different markets and it was presented to Norman and the gang. And that's when they decided to bite at it. But they had to cough up all the money in advance and they wouldn't realize any fruition until August. But they did and of course we really capitalized on it. We milked it for everything it was worth. We had Beatles… everything. And it really catapulted the radio station into number one.

Norman Wain

We dealt with MCA. Brian Epstein was right there and he was

part of it all, but he couldn't make the deals. He was a very nice guy and as a matter fact, he was a little horrified at the dealmakers. I don't remember the guy's name from MCA, but he was the same guy who did this deal in '64. It was the same group that was handling the North American tour.

Not long after WIXY entered the competition for Top 40 listeners in the Cleveland market, Jack Armstrong joined the station's roster of deejays. Known as "Your Leader," his nighttime show became an instant hit thanks to his high energy, rapid-fire delivery style. At 500 words per minute, his talent behind the microphone earned him a spot in *The Guinness Book of World Records* and eventually his own television show in Cleveland. A year later he moved to rival station WKYC, became "Big Jack Armstrong," and has continued his successful career in other major cities throughout the country.

Jack Armstrong

Norman Wain and I had this weird relationship. I was like this surrogate black sheep son when I went to work at WIXY and he would listen to some of the things I had to tell him. He would ignore a lot of the others. But at one point the night show was really taking off and I was doing real well in the ratings. And he said, "I wish we could get the rest of the radio station to jump up like that." And I said, "Bring the Beatles in."

Norman said, "They were here in '64 and there was a riot!"

There were three Top 40 stations and I said, "As popular as the Beatles are now, that would cement your position as THE Top 40 and I think one of the other two will drop out." So they talked it over and decided to pay the front money.

Norman Wain

They needed a big guarantee, which was a problem. We were still a brand new radio station and we were borrowing money. We had to go and get a loan. It was really quite a financial pill for us to swallow.

They wanted money up front – cash. The first time, when we brought them in '64, the guarantee… And by the way, these numbers sound crazy based on today's economics, but the first time we had to have $50,000 up front paid to them. The second time they wanted $75,000. So between '64 and '66, it went up $25,000. For a little station like WIXY, who really wasn't selling that many commercials yet and wasn't really established, seventy-five grand was a major, MAJOR undertaking. We also had to rent Cleveland Stadium.

We had a financial partner by the name of Harry Stone. I'll never forget the meeting where he said, "You're going to spend $75,000, so that's going to bring in $75,000 worth of advertising. Right?"

We said, "Well, no – it's not guaranteed. We're just going to do it for the promotion."

And he said, "What's that gonna do?"

Well it will eventually boost our ratings and then we'll be able to bring in business. In other words, we just knew it was the right thing to do. There was no quid pro quo that it was going to happen as the result of our spending the money and bringing them in.

We knew at that time we were on the right path. We saw what it did for WHK and we were in a three-way battle with WHK and WKYC. Along with WIXY, all three were playing Top 40 music. We just had to do something to break out from the pack and we knew that bringing the Beatles in would be great promotionally for us.

So we rented Cleveland Stadium, thinking we're going to sell 40,000 tickets minimum. That was an 80,000 seat stadium and nobody thought we'd sell 80,000 seats. This was the old Indians baseball stadium and it was huge.

Jerry G. Bishop

I imagine it was a big battle between the radio stations, WHK, WIXY and us. However, WKYC had me on the plane, so it was no contest on air. But somehow the other station owned the rights to introduce them. In 1964 it said, "WHK Presents." In 1966 it was WIXY.

With the concert rescheduled for Municipal Stadium, tickets went on sale in May for $3, $4 and $5, along with box seats at a price almost unheard of for a pop concert at the time, $5.50. Today, unused tickets and ticket stubs are valued at close to $1,000 by collectors. But for teenaged Beatle fans in 1966, their only future investment plan was to raise enough money for a seat at the first rock concert ever held at the Cleveland stadium.

As soon as the news got out, the excitement – the buzz – started building for area Beatle fans who tuned into WIXY for details on where to purchase tickets. In an email to **beatlesincleveland.com**, Marilyn B. recalled her experience the morning tickets went on sale.

Marilyn B

My memory starts with staying at the Stadium in May to purchase Beatles tickets. My girlfriend and I were so excited. We spread out our blankets next to the gate so we could be first in line. I remember the police getting all of our names, phone numbers, addresses, and saying, "If we call your parents, will they know where you are?" I told them yes, but my girlfriend lied and told them her parents were out of town and she was staying at our house. I remember WIXY being down there playing music. At around 5:30 a.m. somebody yelled the ticket counter was opening and everybody in our area got up and stood in line. There was one mother who actually went out and purchased donuts for all of us. With tickets in hand, my girlfriend and I walked back to Terminal Tower and caught the Van Aken Rapid for our happy journey home - sleeping most of the way.

Not long after tickets went on sale, the group's image as lovable mop-tops took a turn in the wrong direction. In America, Capitol Records laid the groundwork for a Beatle Summer by releasing the album, *Yesterday and Today* – with *The Butcher Cover*, in early June. The result was a public relations nightmare. The outcry from shocked parents and record vendors forced Capitol to recall the album and replace the cover with the more subdued photo of The Fab Four lounging around a large traveling case.

In late June, the Beatles were again in the headlines when they performed at Tokyo's Budokan Arena, which was considered a sacred building in Japan and reserved strictly for martial arts. A week later they were accused of snubbing Imelda Marcos, the First Lady of the Philippines, when they failed to attend her private party before a concert in Manila. News photos showed angry demonstrators shouting threats at the Beatles, who were growing tired of the intense spotlight of world fame. Within months they would retreat to their homes in England and the solitude of recording studios for most of their future projects together.

Touring had become dangerous, but before they could isolate themselves from the hysteria of Beatlemania, they were contractually bound for the August tour of North America. With the release of a new album, *Revolver*, and the joyful hit single, *Yellow Submarine*, it was hoped fans would forget about *The Butcher Cover* mishap and not be concerned with what had happened on the other side of the world in Tokyo and Manila. Then *Datebook* hit newsstands and the Beatles were back in the headlines.

Radio stations in the south banned their songs and organized bonfires where Beatle records and other items were burned to protest their U.S. tour. Conservative church leaders preached fire and brimstone against the group, while the Ku Klux Klan burned the Beatles in effigy, nailed their albums to burning crosses, and threatened to disrupt concerts. The warnings and death threats sent a chill not only through the Beatles and their traveling entourage, but also city leaders and police departments assigned to protect them at each stop.

On the eve of their departure, George Harrison was quoted as saying, "Now we have to go to America to get beaten up." With that attitude weighing heavily on their minds, the Beatles' departure was reported in hometown newspapers across the country:

LONDON: The Beatles took off today for their fourth United States tour with Bibles by their seats and a pledge from screaming British fans to "start World War III" if Americans snub them. Hundreds of shaggy-haired London youngsters in hip-hugging pants and mini skirts bid their idols farewell at London Airport in a wild display of support. They threatened to "start World War III" if Americans, upset by Beatle John Lennon's remarks on Christianity, touched a strand on their shaggy heads.

BACK IN THE U.S.

John Lennon
I wasn't saying whatever they're saying I was saying. I was sort of deploring the attitude toward Christianity. From what I've read or observed, it just seems to me to be shrinking and losing contact.

Paul McCartney
And we all deplore the fact.

George Harrison
He really believes in Christianity.

John Lennon
I never meant it as a lousy irreligious thing. I'm sorry.

Jerry G. Bishop
The tour started in Chicago, my home town. When we landed in a city, we would go from an airplane to a hotel. They'd take over a floor or two, like twelve rooms, and then another pack of limos would take us to a ballpark or a concert hall. They'd do the concert,

go back to the hotel and then onto the next city.

I used to carry a tape recorder. Each night on the tour, I would go back to the hotel room and the engineers had given me these clips that were called alligator clips. I'd unscrew the mouthpiece on the phone, clip it on, plug it into the tape recorder and play it back to the station. They edited it back there. I would say it was "Jerry G. on the Beatle Beat." NBC had a regular news service and they used those tapes as well. I was heard all over reporting on this Beatle tour.

The Beatles Are Coming

IN CHICAGO today are the Beatles, England's mop-topped singers. They... assembled in Cleveland Sunday. From top, John Lennon, Paul McCartney, George Harrison and Ringo Starr.

After changing planes in Boston, the Beatles landed in Chicago just after 4 p.m. on Thursday, August 11th, and held a press conference at the Astor Towers Hotel. A visibly nervous Lennon gave a meandering explanation attempting to make sense of his comments, but it was obvious reporters would not be satisfied without an actual apology. After the question was asked pointblank, he officially said he was sorry. Sort of…

John Lennon

If I had said television is more popular than Jesus, I might have got away with it. I'm sorry I opened my mouth. I just happened to be talking to a friend and I used the word "Beatles" as a remote thing. "Beatles" as other people see us. I said they are having more influence on kids and things than anything else. Including Jesus. I said it in that way, which was the wrong way and now it's all this…

I'm not anti-God, anti-Christ, or anti-religion. I was not knocking it. I was not saying we are greater or better. I think it's a bit silly and if they don't like us, why don't they just not buy the records?

Beatle Apologizes for Statement, Claims He Was Misunderstood

On Friday, the media reported his apology and the Beatles performed two shows at Chicago's International Amphitheater. The next day they gave two more concerts at Olympia Stadium in Detroit. Both venues were indoor arenas that held approximately 13,000 fans held in check by a very noticeable police presence.

Jerry G. Bishop

I don't remember the 1966 tour being any different because of John's remarks. Not at all. And I don't think it bothered them. I can remember them going on the air for some news crews to apologize, but it really was a misunderstanding. They didn't know what the hell he meant. That Jesus didn't sell 200 million records? You know? He didn't have 50,000 kids screaming for him? In that sense, in that type of popular, that's all he meant. John didn't mean "we're better than Jesus" or "we are Jesus."

Instead of flying to their next destination, the Beatles ran off stage in Detroit and boarded a Greyhound Bus for the tour's first outdoor stadium show. Although it wasn't in the dreaded Bible Belt, there were concerns about their safety in front of an audience that would number twice as many people than at any of the previous four shows. Snaking its way through a mob of screaming fans, the bus pulled out of the parking lot and headed south to Cleveland.

Following the Ohio Turnpike, they stopped at a plaza in Vermilion, Ohio. From his book, *Ticket To Ride*, Barry Tashian of The

Remains, (one of the four opening acts on the tour), wrote in his journal:

Barry Tashian

Drove in the bus to Cleveland. En route we stopped at a Howard Johnson's, where some people walking by were surprised to see The Beatles out for a stretch near the bus. Arrived in Cleveland at 3 A.M. – tired as hell! I'm going to sleep.

TeenSet Magazine Editor, Judith Sims, was also on the bus, filing reports along the way. From an excerpt reprinted in Tashian's book…

Judith Sims

From Detroit we climbed back on the bus for the ride to Cleveland. Since the bus had remained inside (Olympic) Stadium, there was no James Bondish sort of maneuver getting The Beatles out, as there would be in future adventures. The Beatles dashed from the stage to the bus – complete with stage suits and perspiring brows – and off we went. It was night and the lights were off at first; later I learned that the lights were off because four Beatles were changing clothes in the back of the bus!

It was an all-night ride straight through. At one point the bus pulled off the road in a Howard Johnson's parking lot for a rest stop. Several of us stood outside stretching while Wendy Hanson, Brian Epstein's assistant, went in the restaurant and bought "ice lollies," or ice cream bars, which we promptly consumed. The people inside were completely oblivious to the fact that the lonely betoweled figure sitting on the curb was George Harrison and that the group loitering beside the bus included Paul McCartney, Ringo Starr, Brian Epstein, and so on. A few couples walked by and never even glanced our way – but one woman and two young girls soon came charging up waving paper and pens. They informed Paul that they had been following the bus since Detroit and asked for an autograph. He signed one, after which the woman demanded, "Now sign this one." To which Paul replied, "Is that an order?" She didn't get the hint, but she did get the autographs.

Also included in *Ticket To Ride* is a special memory from a fan. Having a very "tuneful" name made the drive from Detroit more than fab when she actually met Paul McCartney...

Michele

They played in Detroit, then took the Ohio Turnpike to play in Cleveland. Their bus stopped at the Vermilion (Ohio) Turnpike Plaza at 2 a.m., where I met them. Paul sang a shortened version of "Michelle" to me – a thirteen year-old Michele. Imagine!

Ron Sweed

Ernie Anderson had given me an eight millimeter camera for Christmas and I had it with me that night they came to Cleveland. We all went down to the Sheraton Hotel together, but I was independent of our guys at Channel 8. I had a little plan hashed out and I was going to try to get up to the room myself.

The Beatles were on the seventh floor and it was blocked off to the public. You couldn't get up there in the elevators. In fact, one of the detectives told me that when President Kennedy came to Cleveland, the security for the Beatles was more stringent than it was for the President. He couldn't believe this! You've got to keep in mind that these were hardened police force veterans and with the Beatles they were like, "What the hell is going on with this BS?" It wasn't looked upon favorably with all this security and measurements going on for a singing group.

So I made Channel 8 stickers and pasted them on my very unprofessional camera. But the policemen didn't know that. I'd go up to each floor and make friends with whoever was guarding it. You know, "Can I take your picture? This might be on *City Camera News* tonight."

It was stroking everybody's ego and they'd go, "Okay – Yeah!"

They'd stand there and look official and everything. And I was rolling an empty camera because I didn't want to waste film!

I finally got up to the seventh floor and I put my film in the camera. Cleveland deejay, Jerry G. was part of their entourage for this tour and was with them when they came in. The Beatles were waving at me and everything, but my film leader ran through first, so I didn't pick up their actual images until they were past me. There's a shot of Jerry G.'s head, but the best was yet to come anyhow.

Everybody was pretty tired, so they all went to their respective rooms. I knew I'd be back the next day, even though it wasn't going to be an official press conference.

That same evening, as the Beatles arrived in Cleveland, a report went out on the national newswire concerning radio station KLUE in Texas rallying listeners for another Beatle bonfire. The station was struck by lightening during a sudden thunderstorm, damaging their equipment and knocking the station manager unconscious.

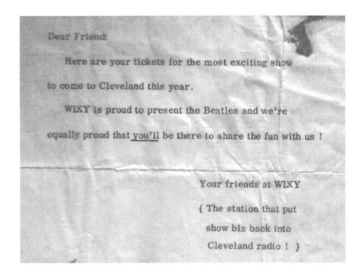

Dear Friend:

Here are your tickets for the most exciting show to come to Cleveland this year.

WIXY is proud to present the Beatles and we're equally proud that you'll be there to share the fun with us !

Your friends at WIXY

(The station that put show biz back into Cleveland radio !)

Beatles Concert
TIX ON SALE HERE!

THE BEATLES-LIVE-IN PERSON
CLEVELAND STADIUM SUNDAY, AUG. 14
7:30 p. m. All Seats Reserved
$3.00 $4.00 $5.00 $5.50
ALSO: "The CYRCLE" "The RONETTES"
"The REMAINS" - Other Exciting Acts
RAIN OR SHINE - Don't Miss this Historic Show!

Jeshen ⬥ Cleveland

Act Two

CLEVELAND, OHIO
Sunday, August 14, 1966

August 14, 1966 was not a typical summer Sunday in Cleveland. Dark clouds, rain, and north winds gusting off Lake Erie chilled the air, making jackets and umbrellas better choices than suntan lotion and beach towels for anyone planning to spend time outside. But the absence of sunshine, heat and humidity is not what makes this date remembered over the past forty years. There was another storm of a different type stirring within the city, keeping it from ever being considered a typical mid-August Sunday.

The Beatles were in Cleveland

SUPER RADIO FOR NORTHERN OHIO ---
WIXY ● 1260
PROUDLY PRESENTS THE FABULOUS
BEATLES
IN CONCERT. IN PERSON.
CLEVELAND STADIUM
7:30 P.M. SUN., AUG 14,1966 — RAIN or SHINE
UPPER STAND
$4.00
NO REFUND

Cleveland Stadium, Cleveland, Ohio, USA

From *The Complete Beatles Chronicle*
by Mark Lewisohn

This one Cleveland concert, at 7:30 pm, like the Public Auditorium show there on 15 September 1964, was held up for 30 minutes when – during the fourth song, 'Day Tripper' – 2500 of the 20,000 fans invaded the Cleveland Indians' baseball field, on which the Beatles were playing.

From *The Beatles*
by Bob Spitz

...in almost every case, the threat of violence was felt. In Cleveland, especially, where an outbreak on the 1964 tour had interrupted the show, there was a repeat performance when three thousand fans rained out of the stands at Municipal Stadium and made a beeline for the stage. The police and Mal Evans, (Beatles road manager), valiantly defended the stage, swatting away marauding fans while the Beatles soldiered on, bashing through "Day Tripper." But at a certain point, as Barrow's, (Tony Barrow, Beatles Press Agent), assistant Bess Coleman observed in *Teen Life*, they were "given the order: Run for your lives! And, did they run!" The boys dropped their instruments mid-song and took off for a trailer stationed behind the home-plate stands, dragging along the frazzled Coleman.

The Cleveland Plain Dealer
August 14, 1966

MEET THE PRESS

At 5:45 p.m., the Beatles had an informal meeting with reporters in one of their rooms on the seventh floor of the Sheraton Cleveland Hotel. Jane Scott covered the event for *The Plain Dealer*.

Jane Scott

This was in what we call now the Renaissance Hotel. It was in a nice room. I was the Teen Editor at *The Plain Dealer*. My whole Saturday page was on teen stuff and I had kids reporting to me from the schools. It was always school stuff like, you know, they have a Peach Festival or something. But after I started writing about the Beatles, nobody wanted anything else on my page but rock. And Harry West, who was editor, really said, "Jane, hit this hard. This is where they live."

I had first heard of them because of *The Ed Sullivan Show*, and I was at the show in 1964 at Public Hall, the first time they came to Cleveland. I wasn't covering it because I wasn't into rock yet. I was still the Teen Editor. Somebody else covered that one. Anyway, I was just so enthused about it and wrote so much about it that I really got tremendous reviews. People were calling about it. So when the time came for their second show in Cleveland, I covered that. I was there. I was the reporter for *The Plain Dealer*.

When I got to the press conference, I was told, "Well, no, we don't need to have you here." So I felt real despondent. Except they did the same thing to their manager! Brian Epstein couldn't get in either! I said, "Well if Brian Epstein can't get in, I'm in good company."

So I went to Norman Wain, who was the head of bringing the Beatles in and he went over and said, "Jane Scott HAS to be here and Brian Epstein is their manager!" And so they let us both in.

Ron Sweed

I had been corresponding with Tony Barrow, one of the Beatles' press officers, and he had sent me a pass for the press conference. It says, "WIXY 1260" on it. But that was before the big problem with the Maureen Cleave interview with John regretting the wane of Christianity and saying the Beatles are more popular with the day's youth than Jesus Christ. When that hit, most of the press conferences were cancelled - including the one in Cleveland.

It wasn't open to the regular press at all and they were just letting the entourage people in. So I went down with our *City Camera* Guys and the Channel 8 News Car, and they were shooting exteriors. It was just all the people and girls around the Sheraton Cleveland, standing ten deep, singing Beatles songs, holding their signs, yelling and screaming and all of that. It was always great Beatlemania that went with their visits.

Again, I have to stress that it was just such a magical time. It really was. I've never been able to experience anything like those three years in the '60's with the Beatles. It was just fantastic.

I was taking eight millimeter shots of the exteriors with the other guys, but then I broke away. I knew they couldn't use eight millimeter on *City Camera*. This was before the days of video, so the only film they would use was sixteen millimeter. The second format they would use was snapshots. They would have thirty-five millimeter pictures or photos that came off the news wires. So whenever they'd do a Beatles story like, "The Beatles are coming," or "They received their MBE Awards," that's usually what they would use, because nine times out of ten the Beatles aren't in town. The camera was just literally shooting this wire photo that was stapled to an easel.

Well, I knew that none of our *City Camera* guys were with the

Beatles. In fact, none of the three Cleveland television stations were up there. So I made my way back to their room again. I saw some lady who was the editor of *TeenSet Magazine*. I also saw Jerry G. and Jane Scott. I barely knew them at this point, but I was in awe of them and they were in there, in addition to the Beatles.

I knew the guys would be back at the TV station by then, so I called just to tell them I was okay and didn't meet them at the car because I was with the Beatles up in their room. And they were like, "Yeah, come on. Where are you really?"

I said, "I'm up here in the Beatles' room – really!" They wanted to know how I did it and I just told them about what I had done the night before and that I was readmitted. I had my eight millimeter, but they asked if the Beatles would let me bring in a camera. I said I didn't know and to hang on.

I had to find someone who was official with the Beatles camp and I think it was Tony Barrow. He had seen me all afternoon and the night before, so it wasn't like a strange face popping up or anything. I asked him if I would be able to run back to the TV station to get a camera so I could shoot some photos. Without a blink of an eye he said, "Sure, go ahead. We'll let you back in."

I went back to the phone and told them it was okay. They told me to take a cab back, have it wait for me, and run up so they could show me how to use the camera. So I went back to the station and they gave me this huge camera, nothing like the small ones that are used today, and said, "Okay, here's all you gotta do. Don't get nervous or anything. If you can stay five or six feet in front of them, that will give us nice close-ups that we'll use on the air. You have twelve shots in the camera."

I got back in the cab, to the hotel, and upstairs with no problem. That's when I rapped off those twelve pictures. I think I did three of each - first John, then Paul, George and Ringo.

Jane Scott

I remember how they sat. Ringo was in the very far back. He was more quiet and not the most popular one to talk to. So first of all I went to John and asked about the comments he made about the Beatles and religion.

"Well," he said, "It's one of those things. You know, it was a private party... They don't think anything about it over there, (England). They just take it with a grain of salt."

He said what he meant was that the church really ought to get together and do more for kids to bring them back in because they weren't going as much. And that they would go to their shows or anything else more than going to church.

Then I asked him how the tour was going. He said, "Well, it's dwindling. You can't expect it to last forever." He admitted the novelty was gone and told me, "Nobody ever said it would go on forever." And that's wrong. It's still going on.

Ron Sweed

I was going around the room and at one point I was sitting right next to John while he was talking. Besides the *TeenSet* lady, there was an English Radio Caroline deejay, Ken Douglas. He was a tall slim guy with a shaggy Beatle haircut and they were very interested in talking about Radio Caroline and stuff.

Revolver had just been released and they were really happy, as everybody was, with the total new direction their sound was going.

And part of the conversation I heard was John lamenting the fact that because of technology being what it was in those days, they couldn't recreate on stage the kind of music they had done on *Revolver*. These were pretty crappy PA systems they had to work off of, so consequently there weren't any synthesizers, monitor speakers, feedback, effects or anything.

John said, "We'd like to do *Yellow Submarine* and everything. Maybe we can get some of those effects if I stick my foot in a

bucket and kick it around or something." He was talking about trying to recreate some of the ambiance in the background that way, but they had to still do the usual set list of songs, including some they did from '64 and '65.

Then that conversation segued into, "Well, this will be it, won't it."

Now, this is not exact, but I'm trying to be careful in what I'm saying here. You know how things go and I think we're all guilty of it, being human beings. Each year that goes by, these stories can get better and better. But sometimes you keep it just as it happened without adding stuff like, "Yeah, and then the Beatles invited me to England and now I'm their best friend and every time they see me they know me and…" You know, I'm really just one of the fifty million people they met.

I'm just trying to tell you that I'm not embellishing this. The conversation did go there – that they were going to stop touring. And I knew before Brian Epstein did because then George said, "Well, did anyone tell Brian then, that this is it for touring?" And I think it was Paul that said, "No, but I guess we'd better."

So there I am, knowing this. I also knew there weren't that many more concerts until their gig in San Francisco and that would be the last time they would tour. And because of that, it spurred me to think, "Well, I may never have the opportunity to see them again."

That's when I whipped out my press pass and figured, "Well, they weren't annoyed that I took twelve pictures today. I'm going to ask them if they'd autograph my press pass." Which they did. They graciously signed it for me. I went to Paul first and he wrote, "Best Wishes – Paul McCartney." Then Ringo – "Ringo Starr" – George Harrison, and John was the last one to sign it.

Jane Scott

Paul was very nice and very talkative. I waited my turn and then asked him about things. I asked him about the girl he was going with. Jane Asher. I asked how that was going and he said, "We're getting to know each other."

I said, "Well, do you have any plans?" And he said, "No. We're just taking it easy. We're taking it quietly. Just getting to know each other and like that."

So we talked and had a nice conversation about The Beatles. "It's getting worse and worse," he said about touring and the criticism about what they played. He said, "If it keeps going like this, we'll have to just have to stop."

Every band needs a Paul. Because Paul has that charm that brings the girls in. John said that about Paul. And I could tell. He was very smiling and everything was very pleasant. He didn't know I was old enough to be his mother, you know! It didn't matter to him. I was just someone to talk to. Later, when Paul came back with Wings, I went upstairs and back stage at Richfield Coliseum. He said I was the only middle-aged person he met during the 1966 tour. He said they were all young people and there I was, a middle aged woman!

Ringo was the oldest, but he didn't look like the oldest. I talked with him just a little bit and I made a mistake, which I've since realized.

He smoked a lot and I asked him what he was smoking. He said it was Lark. I put it in the paper that he smoked Larks and someone who was in advertising said, "Jane, do you realize that you could have gone somewhere and gotten a thousand bucks for that quotation? Do you realize what that would've meant to the Lark people to have a Beatle smoking Larks? And you gave it to them for free? You never should have done it."

I said, "You're right." And I've never done it again. It was a simple thing, but it just shows you how people are very shrewd about those things. But Ringo was very quiet. He didn't say much.

I didn't get much from Harrison. I noticed that he smoked a lot. Every time I saw him he smoked. But it was a nice time. In the background was their manager, Brian Epstein.

Norman Wain

Brian Epstein came to Cleveland. He was here with them. And he was very polite and a very nice guy. Epstein was from a different world. He was soft-spoken, relaxed, trying to be helpful, trying to smooth things over, and trying to make things go well. He was just a gentleman all the way.

Ron Sweed

I've been around and in television stations since I was thirteen at Channel 8 and you meet your share of very nice people. You also meet your share of people that are full of themselves. I have to include as some of the nicest people in a situation where it could have really gone to their heads, were the Beatles.

They were just four guys from Liverpool who were totally middle class and luckily had the right breaks. I mean, they had the talent and then the right breaks brought that talent to the worldwide spotlight. But they never lost the sense of just being four guys with an incredible sense of humor. That's what's always attracted me to people is a sense of humor. Also a lack of ego. I mean you have to have an ego to know you have that kind of talent, or any kind of talent, but you don't act like you're better than someone else.

I think that coupled with the fact that I was fourteen, fifteen and sixteen when I met them. Now remember, they were just eighteen and nineteen going into this, so the disparity in ages was relatively small. We all had a common bond in that we loved rock'n roll music.

I knew American music inside and out. I was living and breathing it every day and one of their most passionate interests was American rock and roll music. And we talked about it. George and I talked about Lou Christie and some of the other songs that were in the Top Ten at the time. It was as interesting to them to hear my views about what was going on with the American performers, just as it was for me to hear their input.

George Harrison, just to show you where their heads were at, couldn't wait to get back home, because he felt it was integral that he practice his guitar some more after these live tours. He was not satisfied with where he was at as a musician yet. I mean, imagine someone in their position thinking they weren't good enough at the time.

Jerry G. Bishop

I was about the same age as the Beatles and that's why we related. I think if you listen to our interviews you'll hear that we got along pretty well.

I was closest to Paul. He and I really hit it off. George was... I mean, it was just like their labels. George was the quiet one. Ringo was about as smart as your average ash tray. He was pleasant, but not a rocket scientist.

John was the most thoughtful of all of them about the condition the world was in. Even then, he hadn't come out politically yet, but I could see little flashes of him giving a shit. Paul was just a good'ol boy, screwing everything that walked. Not that they all didn't, but...

 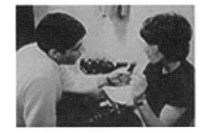

Have you ever been to Liverpool? Don't bother. It's Cleveland, but much worse.

No offense to Cleveland. I was back last year and I was very impressed. I thought the city would've really taken off when they got the Rock'n Roll Museum, Jacob's Field, (new baseball stadium), and the downtown redevelopment. But I drove down Euclid Avenue from Cleveland Heights and that whole strip is just desolate. Multiply that to a whole city and it's Liverpool. It's a seaport town and it's just the same. The boats come in and they take the stuff and put it on a train and get it out of there. So the guys who work there are just working stiffs. That's what the Beatles would've been, except they got lucky. In more ways than one.

Jane Scott

Anyway, when these reporters come with their microphones, they put them right in front of somebody and you have to sort of wait a bit. That's the reason I got to John right away because he was really the reason why I was there. Plus the fact they were all around Paul a little bit. That's why.

John's quote was the only reason I was there. And there were stories about people in various places that were tossing Beatles records out the window. It was just a publicity stunt. They didn't give a damn. They got their picture taken tossing it out of a window. You know, saying that we don't like someone who thinks they're better than God or something like that. Of course that was a lot of bull, because they just wanted the publicity too. We saw through that. I didn't really see it around Cleveland.

The press conference seemed to go pretty long. Of course they finally came around and said, "Time."

Jerry G. Bishop

That worked out great for me. We had a camera crew following us around, but I'm sure that footage is not anywhere to be found. It would've been the News Department at Channel 3 because my show was on that channel and I was on the sister radio station. So I didn't go to the concert, because I had seen twenty Beatles concerts and never heard them sing. I went back to the station to edit audio and video.

I had no real reason to go. I had heard them sing in hotel rooms, dressing rooms and around a pool with acoustic guitars, which is the way to hear them. But when you went to a concert you couldn't hear them. If they were standing right in front of you, you wouldn't hear them sing because of the noise. The din was ear-splitting from half an hour before they walked on stage to a half hour afterwards.

Despite the conversation between John, Paul and George about not touring anymore, they were not ready to make an announcement to the rest of the world. In fact, they ended the informal press conference saying the Beatles would be back again in 1967.

It was planned in advance that Jerry G. would leave the tour in Cleveland because of commitments to both his radio and television shows. On his CD, *Beatletalk*, which is a compilation of interviews he did with the band during the 1965 and 1966 tours, they each recorded a good-bye message in Cleveland, before posing with Bishop for a final photo.

John Lennon

Good-bye to the, you know, the USA. It's been great and we'll be back again next year, if you still want us. And we'll probably see you next year.

Paul McCartney

(To Jerry G. Bishop). You'll have to come on the next one. It's just a good laugh, the tour, you know. It's good. We've enjoyed having you with us.

George Harrison

It's almost definite that we'll be back around the same time next year. And so if you didn't see us this time, maybe you'll see us next time – if you want to. And I hope you do. All those who don't want to see us… never mind.

Perhaps the Beatles hadn't made a final decision to stop touring, but it was a subject they had talked about in Cleveland. They were less than two months removed from the events in Tokyo and Manila; the backlash caused by *The Butcher Cover*, and were forced to deal with Lennon's comments about religion on a daily basis in America. There were still two weeks left on the tour, which would include more death threats, hysterical fans, and even the danger of electrical shock from guitars and microphones while performing outside during thunderstorms.

It's doubtful anyone could have predicted what was about to

happen that evening - or if it would play a part in their actual decision to stop touring. As the Beatles left for their suites to prepare for the concert, anxious fans were already waiting for them at Cleveland Municipal Stadium.

WIXY®1260

CLEVELAND, OHIO

Cordially invites you to attend the exclusive

BEATLES PRESS CONFERENCE

TIME: 5:45 PM - SUNDAY, AUGUST 14, 1966

PLACE: THE EMPIRE ROOM, PARLOR FLOOR
SHERATON-CLEVELAND HOTEL

NOTE: This invitation is extended for the sole personal use of

_____

and cannot be transferred to anyone else. Conference is designed for working press only and will start on time. Doors will close at 6:00 PM sharp. No one will be admitted to conference room after it starts. Should you wish to set up equipment earlier, the room will be open for your use beginning at 3:00 PM. This ticket is solely for admission to the Press Conference. This ticket does not allow you into backstage or dressing room areas at the Stadium, and is not good for admission to the Press Box or any other seat at the Stadium.

NO.

FANS, SOUND AND A LUXURY TRAILER

A few blocks away from the hotel, excitement was building as fans arrived at Municipal Stadium for the 7:30 p.m. show. Ignoring the wind and light rain, vendors sold Beatle pennants and buttons in the parking lots, while through the turnstiles fans could purchase official tour programs for $1 each.

Norman Wain

We thought we'd sell 40,000 or 50,000 seats. But about a month before the Beatles came in, John Lennon made that unfortunate remark that the Beatles were bigger than Christ. He explained it to us and what he meant was that he himself was shocked at the Beatles phenomenon. He couldn't believe that they were being accepted and were as big as they were. He felt they were just another band. He didn't think they were anything so special.

And remember, this was before *Sgt. Pepper* and when they got into the really philosophic things. This is still the days of "She loves you, yeah, yeah, yeah." The simplistic songs. You know what I'm saying. But they were really big. They were actually bigger than they thought they were.

There's no question John's remark hurt ticket sales. They were going pretty well and then all of sudden, it stopped. The Archdiocese in Cleveland – I forget the name of the Bishop at the time – came out with a statement. He didn't ban Catholics from going, but what he said was "Good Catholics aren't going to go to that show." It was something like that.

In Cleveland, Reverend Thurman H. Babbs had threatened to excommunicate any member of his congregation who not only attended, but also listened to the Beatles. Outside the stadium on the day of the show, a small group of religious protestors were stationed near the southwest gates urging fans to boycott the show.

Norman Wain

He just said it's not a great idea to go to that show, because he's disparaging Christ. So all of a sudden, ticket sales really stopped. Well, we did everything possible. We went to Erie, Pennsylvania and we tried to get the radio stations there to promote it. We went down to Youngstown, Akron and Sandusky. We tried like crazy to arrange for people to come in to see the show. We think there was somewhere between 20,000 to 25,000 people there that day. The number we gave out to the press was 25,000. I think there were maybe 20,000 people.

Jack Armstrong

John Lennon had said that the Beatles were more popular than Christ, at least on an international basis. He was misquoted, basically. But it didn't make any difference. Fundamentalist Christians went crazy and they started burning Beatle albums, breaking records and all kinds of stuff. All the Beatle music came off the radio in cities in Louisiana, Alabama and places like that. And it really hurt the ticket sales in Cleveland.

The other thing that hurt ticket sales was that they were at a low point in recorded music. The stuff they had out really wasn't startling anymore. This was before *Sgt. Pepper*. So what you had was that tailing out of Beatle material. And of course up to that moment, a lot of groups had four or five hit records in a row and then just disappeared. So it looked like the Beatles might fade out a little bit and they came to town on a low note.

Norman Wain

The guy we booked the Beatles through at MCA was with them in Cleveland. The first thing he said to me when I met him at the stadium for the concert was, "Hey, can I buy back my introduction to you guys?" He had heard about the problem with the Catholic Diocese.

So he says, "You had a riot in '64 and now you got this in '66. Can I buy back my introduction to you guys?" You know?

He was one of these "d'ees, d'ems and do'sers." He was a typical Broadway... I don't want to say charlatan, but he was a sharpie - a Broadway sharpie. He had the diamond cufflinks and the white on white shirt and the whole business.

Inside the stadium, a stage approximately five feet in height had been constructed over second base on the baseball infield. Since the concert would be held "rain or shine," sheets of blue plastic were framed on three sides and over the top of the stage before the show to protect the Beatles and their equipment from the weather.

The sound system for the show would be impressive today, if it were held indoors at a small theater. "Super Beatle" Vox Amplifiers almost six feet tall would power the guitars from the rear of the stage, while Ringo's drum kit sat just behind on a four foot riser. The technology for using monitors or speakers placed in front of the group so they could hear a mix of how the vocals and music sounded together hadn't been developed by 1966, so John, Paul and George could only rely on what came out of the amplifiers behind them. Ringo would attempt to follow the beat by watching how the others moved or tapped their feet.

The vocal microphones could not be powered through amplifiers at the back of the stage without causing feedback. This effect, used by Lennon on his guitar as the opening note of *I Feel Fine*, can best be described as a "circular motion." For the Beatles to be facing the audience, their microphones had to be aimed toward their mouths, which meant the microphones were also aimed toward the amplifiers at the rear of the stage. In this configuration, the microphones would not only pick up the vocals, but also the guitars coming from the Super Beatle Amplifiers behind them. Eventually the audio mixture of vocals and guitars would run through the microphones, out of the amplifiers, through the microphones, out of the amplifiers again – and continue until developing into a high-pitched electronic squeal that worked on *I Feel Fine*, but would undoubtedly have everyone in the stadium holding their ears and screaming for silence.

The Beatles's vocals were carried through two tables of speakers placed along the first and third baselines of the baseball infield, approximately half way toward the stands. It's doubtful the group could hear what they were singing, since these speakers were aimed at the fans and not toward the stage. The idea was to keep the vocal and guitar speakers so one didn't overpower the other, while all the Beatles could do was keep their guitar and drum playing together and hope what they shouted into the microphones was at least heard by the fans.

But in the huge expanse of the open stadium, this sound system was hardly big enough to overpower the screams from thousands of fans. The microphones and amplifiers were also connected into the public address system and carried through small speakers hanging from support beams throughout the stadium. Designed for short, halting announcements that would echo through the stands during sports events, this resulted in a delay of at least a few seconds until fans would actually hear what had been played on stage.

Norman Wain

It's so unbelievable. All we had was normal amplification. The guitars, of course, were amplified and the guys were singing into the mics. In other words, they had microphones on stands on the floor and they picked up the sound of the guitars behind them. And there were exactly four people on stage with just some lights. That was it - three guitarists and singers, with Ringo Starr in the back. There was no production. No big smoke bombs going off. They didn't even have stage monitors.

You could hear them okay, but it wasn't this big booming – you know, blow you out of your seats sound that you have today.

Behind the stage and toward first base was a white "luxury" house trailer provided by a local businessman, Phil Braff, to advertise his Sahara Mobile Home Park in North Madison. The trailer was fifty feet long and ten feet wide, and would serve as a soundproof dressing room where the Beatles could relax, listen to the radio, or even take a nap while the opening acts performed.

Norman Wain

We had a little portable stage right there at second base. And right behind it we rented a trailer – you know, a mobile home – to act as back stage for the performers. That's where those pictures were taken. Right there with Jack Armstrong and some of our disk jockeys.

Johnny Canton:

This guy came to us and said, "You might need a green room or something like that. I'd be happy to supply you with a trailer, mobile home, whatever." He customized it and it was gorgeous. It was beautiful – right there at second base. That's where we sat and had some pictures taken and chatted with the Beatles.

In 1966, Joe Stipe was an employee of Braff's at Sahara Mobile Home Park. He was responsible for the trailer and was waiting inside to greet the Beatles.

Joe Stipe:

I didn't drive the trailer in myself. I had one of my men do it and had three other men help me set it up. We pulled into the stadium and it sat off second base. It had air conditioning and all kinds of stuff for them to drink and eat - sandwiches and bottles of pop.

The trailer was really nice. It didn't have a TV, but it had a radio. Then they had speakers all over the place. And each Beatle had his own color. It had four different colors of chairs. The whole thing had white carpeting and there was a zebra couch. We had all kinds of big pictures on the walls from England. They were really nice, but somebody later stole most of them. People broke into it over the years and stole different stuff from it.

Each one had his own bedroom in the back. They didn't have time to sleep, but it was made as if they would stay all night. Each room had two little half beds and each one had their own covers, with different colors for each bed. There was a full bathroom that had all the colors too. It was fifty feet long and ten feet wide. That was as big as they made them at that time.

That morning, *The Plain Dealer* carried photos and an article about the trailer written by a young journalist, Jeannie Simons. Today the author is better known as Jeannie Emser, Director of Public Relations for Cleveland's Playhouse Square Theater District:

Jeannie Simons

One look at the thick white plush carpeting is enough to make the Fab Four jump out of their boots and run barefoot on the floors... or walls, for that matter, since the plush extends to the ceilings, even in the bathroom. This  elegance is continued throughout the dressing room with black plush chairs and a zebra couch in the living room.

Over 20,000 fans filled the upper and lower sections inside the stadium facing the small stage. To protect the Beatles, the city had assigned a small group of policemen, many in riot gear with white helmets and wooden nightsticks.

Norman Wain

We had a secondary problem in that the police were bemused over it and didn't exactly watch the crowd the way they should. And another thing, all we had was the police themselves. We had no security outside of what the Cleveland Police Department thought was adequate. There were maybe fifteen to twenty policemen. It could have been a little more, but I don't think so. Whatever it was, they were supplied by the Cleveland Police Department and we didn't hire anybody special.

As added security, a snow fence made of thin wooden slats held together with wire and standing four feet tall, was stretched between the stands and the baseball infield. Designed to prevent snow from drifting over roads during winter storms, it was hoped the fence could also keep any overexcited fans from getting too near the stage.

Ron Sweed

When we got there, I saw this little snow fence, which is what they had for security. That and a handful – a sporadic sprinkling – of policemen. I told our press guys that it wasn't gonna hold anybody back. I said, "I guarantee it won't hold anybody back." I was genuinely disturbed over the lack of forethought that went into this.

Jack Armstrong

That night, Norman was really upset, because they had just barely broken even on the concert. I think he breathed a sigh of relief because it looked like they were going to actually break even. But that was not the purpose of it.

Norman Wain

It was just a big exciting evening. And it was more or less successful. We could have sold more tickets. But we got what we wanted out of it anyway, because there was all the buzz and the talk and excitement ahead of time and for weeks afterwards. So it meant "tune in to the radio station." Remember, what we were looking for were listeners. We didn't want to make money on the concert. We weren't concert promoters.

As a matter of fact, the experience led us to talk with Belkin Productions later on and work out a partnership with them where we said, "Look, you guys bring in the acts. You lay out the money and you keep the profit. All we want is our sign there and our deejays there."

Because what was of value to us was the buzz, because the buzz meant tune-in. Tune-in meant ratings and ratings meant business. So all we wanted was the notoriety and the fame – and good fortune would follow.

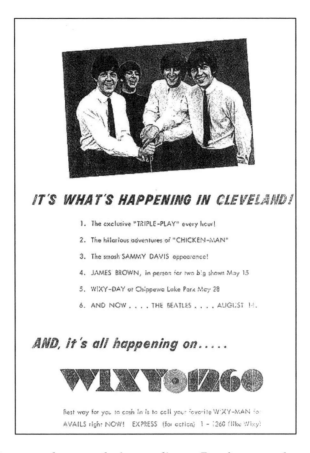

IT'S WHAT'S HAPPENING IN CLEVELAND!

1. The exclusive "TRIPLE-PLAY" every hour!

2. The hilarious adventures of "CHICKEN-MAN"

3. The smash SAMMY DAVIS appearance!

4. JAMES BROWN, in person for two big shows May 15

5. WIXY-DAY at Chippewa Lake Park May 28

6. AND NOW . . . . THE BEATLES . . . . AUGUST 14.

AND, it's all happening on . . . . .

WIXY 1260

Best way for you to cash in is to call your favorite WIXY-MAN for AVAILS right NOW! EXPRESS (for action) 1 - 1260 (like Wixy!

As the crowd entered the stadium, *Revolver*, was heard blaring through the sound system. As a testament to the days of vinyl records, (for a full explanation, see *Introduction To Albums 101* in this book's Preface), only side two was played repeatedly since no one bothered to turn the album over.

I Me Mine

Whether it was just good fortune or the gods of rock'n roll offering a prelude for the "Don't rain!" chant at Woodstock three years later, one of the songs heard numerous times as the second side of *Revolver* was played over and over was *Good Day Sunshine*. As I was reminded during my drive through Cleveland's West Side Market forty years after this experience, the song will forever have a personal history of chasing away any summertime blues that can be brought on by cold and damp weather.

Just before the show was scheduled to begin, the rain stopped. Good day sunshine!

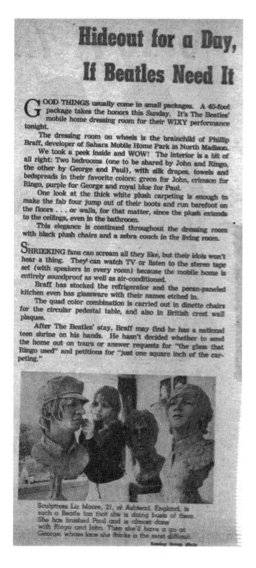

Hideout for a Day, If Beatles Need It

GOOD THINGS usually come in small packages. A 40-foot package takes the honors this Sunday. It's The Beatles' mobile home dressing room for their WIXY performance tonight.

The dressing room on wheels is the brainchild of Phillip Braff, developer of Sahara Mobile Home Park in North Madison.

We took a peek inside and WOW! The interior is a bit of all right: Two bedrooms (one to be shared by John and Ringo, the other by George and Paul), with silk drapes, towels and bedspreads in their favorite colors: green for John, crimson for Ringo, purple for George and royal blue for Paul.

One look at the thick white plush carpeting is enough to make the fab four jump out of their boots and run barefoot on the floors . . . or walls, for that matter, since the plush extends to the ceilings, even in the bathroom.

This elegance is continued throughout the dressing room with black plush chairs and a zebra couch in the living room.

SHRIEKING fans can scream all they like, but their idols won't hear a thing. They can watch TV or listen to the stereo tape set (with speakers in every room) because the mobile home is entirely soundproof as well as air-conditioned.

Braff has stocked the refrigerator and the pecan-paneled kitchen even has glassware with their names etched in.

The quad color combination is carried out in dinette chairs for the circular pedestal table, and also in British crest wall plaques.

After The Beatles' stay, Braff may find he has a national teen shrine on his hands. He hasn't decided whether to send the home out on tours or answer requests for "the glass that Ringo used" and petitions for "just one square inch of the carpeting."

Sculptress Liz Moore, 21, of Ashtead, England, is such a Beatle fan that she is doing busts of them. She has finished Paul and is almost done with Ringo and John. Then she'll have a go at George, whose face she thinks is the most difficult.

BACKSTAGE WITH THE BEATLES

Just before 7:30 p.m., the gates in right field were opened and four identical limousines drove slowly into the stadium. Fans stood and filled the air with loud screams as the cars headed onto the infield and stopped in front of the trailer.

For security reasons, three of the limos had been used as decoys while transporting the group from their hotel. As John, Paul, George and Ringo stepped out of the same car and waved to the crowd, another burst of adrenaline swept through the stadium. The high-pitched squeals continued until they disappeared into the trailer.

Jack Armstrong

We all had on WIXY jackets and I was out around second base where the trailer was. Norman came by and I had a Beatles program. I said, "Norm, can I get in and talk to the Beatles and have them sign my program?"

And he said, "NO!" He yelled at me. "NO!" He said, "BUT, you are the MC of this damn show." And then he went on into the trailer.

I thought, "I'm the WHAT?" I had no knowledge whatsoever that I was going to have to do anything but stand out there on the stage and say, "Hi," and get off the stage and watch the Beatles. So I was the MC and… what a sweat!

We went into the trailer to wait for the Beatles. They let all of us in – Bob Engle, Al Gates, Johnny Canton… We were all in there.

The door opened and in came their body guard and then the

Beatles behind him. But I distinctly remember seeing the Beatles and thinking, "Gee, isn't that funny. Look – there's four midgets who look like the Beatles." Because they were very short and they were very slight.

You have a tendency to think everybody in show business is John Wayne. And when you meet them you find... Elvis seemed like a short guy for cryin' out loud, because I'm six foot two. So when they came in I was startled. I was like, "Oh my God, it is the Beatles but they're smaller than I thought."

I've met a lot of people, and I had met a lot of people up to that moment, but it physically affected me when they came into the room. The hair on the back of my head stood up. I don't know why. I have said this in the past when people have asked me about it. I said I thought the hand of God was in the room.

They really did change everything. I mean they really were THE force in music as long as they were together. But I didn't have any hero worship, so it wasn't like that. It was like there was something phenomenal going on there. And since then, I had met them individually and there wasn't the same feeling. It was just the four of them together that produced that kind of reaction.

Norman Wain

I don't know if it was real or imagined, but they said, "Oh hi!" You know, like they recognized us from before. I don't know if they really remembered us, but they certainly remembered being in Cleveland, the 10,000 seat Public Hall with the riot and all that stuff. But whether they knew Norman Wain, Bob Weiss or Joseph Zingale, I can't guarantee. But they certainly made out like they did.

The funny part was that they weren't any different than they were two years earlier. They'd had a lot of experiences since then. They had traveled the world, but they were still the unassuming kids from Liverpool. They were still amazed that their music and their appearance could create that hysteria. And that's the one thing I really truly remember about them. They hadn't gone "showbiz." They hadn't gone "Big Time." They weren't saying, you know, "I need this, I need that..." They were very, very unassuming, modest types – just

the way they were in '64 and it was amazing to me that they were that way.

Joe Stipe

The crowd had been very orderly and then all at once they went crazy. Then the Beatles walked in the trailer. I was sitting in there with them and we had a great time just talking. We were there for about an hour before they started. It had good sound insulation, so we didn't have a problem with the noise.

They were real nice boys. They came in wearing regular pants and shirts, but before they went on stage they put on their suits and everything. Of course they got all made up, like anytime you have a stage show or a movie or anything else.

They had their guitars and I got a set of strings because they broke one. Ringo gave them to me and I had them for a long time. They tuned up their guitars real nice and everything. Then they said, "Okay," and just set them up against the wall.

We talked about where the mobile home had come from, where they lived in England, and how they got started. They got started as just a small little band, because they thought it would be a fun thing to do. And then they got so big they went all around the world.

Johnny Canton

Paul McCartney is my age and at that time we were all in our twenties. And they were just fun. We didn't talk about anything specific. Not really. You know, nothing more than, how are you enjoying America? "We love it."

We talked about their touring. They were busy and everybody was at them. But they were very personable, as I remember. There wasn't any star treatment. Not really. They didn't seem into that, even though, obviously, they had limousines bring them out to second base and to the trailer and all that. They were just fun loving. They were having a good time.

Norman Wain

They spoke with these deep British accents. I guess the accent is not London, it's the countryside and they felt that they were sort of like... I think they pictured themselves as country bumpkins who hit it lucky. I really feel that way about it.

But I will say this; it was around this time that John and Paul were starting to write other stuff. It wasn't long afterwards that they came out with those beautiful albums, *Sgt. Pepper* and *The White Album*, because they were deepening their ability to perform good music.

Jack Armstrong

So at any rate we got a picture with them and all the WIXY jocks on the couch. Then I pulled out my trusty program that I wanted to have signed for my wife to be, who was Wendy in Chapel Hill, North Carolina. I was going to get married to her about a year after that and I wanted to have them sign, "To Wendy, Ringo Starr..." and that kind of stuff. I asked them while I was sitting on the couch.

I asked Lennon, I said, "John could you guys sign a program for my future wife?" He said, "Oh, of course Jack. No problem." And he wrote half a paragraph!

Norman Wain

I took a couple of those pictures, and a photographer took some of the others. My son hates the fact that I never got in front of the camera.

They were pictures of the guys wearing red jackets. We had WIXY jackets. You know, in those days the deejays had sort of uniforms.

Jack Armstrong

While he was signing his picture, I noticed there was some shuffling going on. I looked up and everybody was out. They had taken everybody else, including Norman, out of the trailer. I was the only one in the trailer with them.

They passed the program around and each of them wrote little things. And by the way, I saw that she sold that program at an auction for $75,000. And of course we're long divorced...

I said, "Thank you very much," and then we talked. They wanted to know something about Cleveland and I said it was an industrial

town. They wanted to know how their music was doing and I said it was doing well. I also said the latest releases were not as strong as the earlier stuff and they said, "We know."

But that's the way it was back then. We were all professionals and it was how we all looked at what we did. They were really interested in what everyone thought of their music and if the fans liked it as much as their earlier stuff. They also wanted to do a good show; just like I wanted to be the best MC I could be when I put them on stage. It was all very professional.

And it was also not on the basis at all of, "We're stars and you're nothing." Later on when you had super groups like Led Zeppelin and things like that, they wouldn't even let you on stage. You couldn't go out and introduce them, because they felt they were in a whole different stratosphere than you were. The Beatles didn't have an ounce of that.

I think they had done some homework and realized how important the deejays were in America. They knew that there were hundreds of Top 40 stations and they were the keys to everything. The Beatles treated us as if we were the keys. And we really were. We had a lot more freedom back then. They wanted to keep us on their side.

Jerry G. Bishop

I went to *The Ed Sullivan Show* with the Beatles in 1965. We had a little limo convoy and they took us all, including Murray The K. You know that name? Major asshole – and you can quote me on that. They hated him. But he was a powerful disk jockey in New York, so they had to be sort of nice to him. They still thought they had to be nice to the media. They didn't realize it was the other way around. They didn't realize that they were bigger than anybody in the media. In 1965 they were just at that point where, "Man, I'm really hot stuff!" But they hadn't totally figured it out yet. We knew it. Murray The K didn't: "Well, they need me!" You know?

Jack Armstrong

It was really a professional relationship between the jocks and the groups. It was not one of those hero worship things. And they're the ONLY group and the ONLY people that I have ever worked with, and I've worked with just about everybody, that I asked to sign a program. I never did that with anybody else. I thought that was really like a low rent thing to do to an act. You know, to say, "I really love your music, so would you sign this program…" I didn't have any autograph books or anything like that. There was a professional point of view and that's it.

At any rate, Lennon and I were talking about radio and about what was going on. He was by and far not only the smartest one of the group, but the obvious leader. What he said went and it was as simple as that. He was the most organized and very alert.

McCartney drifted over to a chair and picked up *The Wall Street Journal* and started reading it. That was an indication to me that McCartney thought the group wasn't going to last forever and he was going to make the most out of the money they were making. That's what I got out of that. And that was probably good business sense.

What I got from Lennon was that he didn't give a damn. He just didn't care. I mean he was bright enough... He had been called attention to in a super group and that was all he was ever gonna need. And he was probably right. Because he had so much talent and it

was, you know, going to be endless. And that's basically what it was.

Ringo and Harrison went in the back of the trailer. There were some older women that came in with them. I don't know who the hell they were. But they went in the back of the trailer and I smelled burning leaves for the first time in my life. I didn't even know what it was because I had never done marijuana. Then I said, "Well, I have to go and put the acts on."

Norman Wain

Ringo and George always played a secondary role. Anytime we would talk to the four of them, it was always Paul and John who answered the questions and who were more forthcoming about anything.

They also had a great sense of humor. I wish the hell I'd had a tape recorder there in both 1964 and '66. They had a wry sense of humor and even a self-deprecating sense of humor. I remember John said, "I imagine any one of those girls would be glad to share my bed."

I mean, it's like they couldn't believe what was going on! They were just amazed about it, you know? They seemed to me like young guys who were just in the eye of a storm and the storm was all around them, but not with them.

Joe Stipe

Before the show, we had a big sign on top of the trailer that said, Sahara Mobile Homes. But the Beatles said to take that sign down or they wouldn't go on stage. They said they wouldn't do a show beneath anybody's sign. That was their way of doing it. They had that authority to say what they wanted, you know. So we had to take the sign down and put it on the back of the mobile home.

They also made me an offer to buy the trailer. The owner wanted $75,000 for it and the Beatles offered me $50,000. Well, I didn't have the owner around to say if he would take less. I tried to call him, but he was out.

A few days or so later, I got back in touch with the Beatles and they were in Boston or something. I asked if they would still be interested. They said, "No, we would've bought it that night." They said they couldn't give over $50,000, but since we didn't get back to them while they were here, now it would be in their way. They said it was too late.

We used to show the mobile home at the Sahara Mobile Homes Park and charge fifty cents to go through it. And we took it to the county fair and a couple other fairs. There wasn't any money to be made because you had to have so many guards around to keep people from tearing it up.

They were just ordinary, common guys while they were sitting inside. They were all looking out of the window to see what was going on in the stadium. I was surprised because I thought they'd be biggity, but they weren't. They were just nice young men.

Norman Wain

One of the questions they asked was, "How are we gonna get out of here?" And we explained to them that at the end of the concert we were going to spirit them away with the double Cadillac Limousines deal. The first limousine would get the kids' attention and they would run after that. Then the Beatles would leave in a second limousine.

They were very happy about that, because they were a little concerned. I guess they'd had some close scrapes in other stadiums.

You gotta understand the public, the police, the security and the performers were still learning at this time. It wasn't long afterwards that big acts would come in and draw 80,000 people and everybody knew how to handle everything because it had progressed.

The WIXY deejays in their matching maroon blazers walked on stage to start the first ever rock'n roll concert at Cleveland Municipal Stadium. It was 7:30 on a damp, windy evening and the Beatles were waiting in the trailer for their turn to perform. The fans were just starting to warm up…

OPENING ACTS

Each of the opening acts on the Beatles 1966 tour has earned their own place in pop music history. Not only because they shared the stage with the Beatles, but because of their contributions to the music scene. Three of the four had big hits in 1966 that are still played on the radio to this day, while the "remaining" act appeared later that summer on *The Ed Sullivan Show*.

The first group introduced by the WIXY deejays –and therefore, the first rock performers to ever perform at Cleveland Municipal Stadium - was The Remains, a hot club band out of Boston. They were also known as Barry and the Remains after the founder of the group, Barry Tashian.

More than thirty years later they were mentioned in the book *Walk This Way: The Autobiography Of Aerosmith* as one of the area's most popular groups that also had the stellar reputation that came from touring with the Beatles. The band had numerous regional hits, including *Don't Look Back*, and appeared on *The Ed Sullivan Show* and NBC's *Hullabaloo* in 1966. The Remains were obviously competent musicians who, once they finished their twenty minute set, "remained" on stage to back up Bobby Hebb and The Ronettes.

Not long after this tour, the group disbanded with Tashian moving more into country and rhythm & blues styles of music. He recorded with Gram Parsons and was an original member of The Flying Burrito Brothers. For ten years in the 1980's he was a member of The Hot Band, which backed Emmylou Harris. He later joined his wife Holly in recording and touring the world with their own group. In 1996 his book *Ticket To Ride* was published to commemorate the thirtieth anniversary of his tour with The Beatles. He currently lives in Nashville and has regrouped The Remains for shows that have been earning rave reviews from both music critics and fans.

Barry Tashian

We were in the right place at the right time. Our manager in New York happened to have contact with the agency that was putting the tour together. And one day he just came into the office and said, "You guys want to go on The Beatles tour? I can get you in there if you want." So it was pretty much dropped in our lap, amazingly enough.

I vaguely remember taking the bus from Detroit to Cleveland. We stopped... George and I had formed a club where we'd get out and smoke together. That was fun. He was nice to me. He didn't have to be, but he was. George was the Beatle I got closest to. Absolutely. I had a good time chatting with him almost every day on the flights and sometimes visiting with him in his room. We'd listen to some sitar music and just kind of hang out.

Paul was the most stand-offish. He wasn't really interested in any of us.

I'd say the stereotypes that people have of the Beatles are pretty much like their film, *A Hard Day's Night*. You know, it was written around their characters and I think as you see them in that film is pretty much what I perceived as their personalities.

This tour was very strange in a way, because in the center of everything - where we were - it was very quiet. All the press people who were on the plane probably made it seem more of an event than anything. But just strictly traveling together, it was very quiet and calm. It was like being in the eye of a hurricane, I guess, because they were about as popular as you could get in the world.

Of course at the venues, forget it. There was just so much going on I didn't even try to get close to them or even go in their dressing rooms or anything like that. But as far as being on a bus or on the plane, or standing outside the plane at night before taking off, it all seemed very, kind'a weirdly, intimate and quiet.

At the Cleveland concert, we weren't in the trailer. We came out of the dugout along the third base side. Our dressing rooms were mostly on the visiting team side, so we came out of there.

We played twenty minutes. We went on first and played our own set. Then we backed Bobby Hebb for twenty minutes or so. He sang *Sunny*. Then The Cyrkle came up and played. During their set, we probably went back to the dugout, unless we hung out behind the stage just for their twenty minutes, because we had to go back on stage to back-up The Ronettes. And then, the Beatles...

I didn't want to perform as a back-up band at first. But it was such a big opportunity to be on that tour that we just ended up saying, "Alright, we'll do it!" I was just trying to fulfill my obligations.

We left Cleveland Stadium that night before the Beatles came on. It wasn't a good night, (for The Remains). I wasn't having fun, there was an opportunity to go back to the hotel and I just said, "Let's go." So we went back. That night in my journal I wrote:

"The stadium is huge. It felt so strange being out on a baseball field. The stage is behind second base, too far from the audience. The nearest person was at least one hundred and twenty feet away. I felt like we had no contact with them at all. We could hardly see them and they could hardly see us, or so it seemed. What a drag. Hope the people felt differently about it. At least the weather warmed up some. Returned to the Statler Hilton right after our show. Didn't stay to see The Beatles. There was some ruckus outside the stadium. I wanted to get out of there."

I don't remember too much about that show. I just remember leaving right after we played, thinking we did a terrible show. It was the first time we played at a huge outdoor place. The Chicago and Detroit shows were both indoors. This was the first outdoor ball field. And it was a damp, cloudy night, so maybe the speakers were all kind of wet and everything sounded funny. If it affected the playing, it probably affected it in a negative way.

At the indoor places, the audience was up close so we felt like we were maybe communicating with people. But in Cleveland, all of a sudden we were on second base. The closest person was a hundred and twenty-five feet away. So, as if we didn't have a tough enough job being relatively unknown and going on before The Beatles, all of a sudden now we're dealing with all this distance too. So it was really kind of a shock for us. That first show was Cleveland.

You couldn't really make out anybody's face in the audience; the individual features of people's faces. It was just kind of anonymous. And with all the lights on, it looked like you were just out there in space playing. So that was kind of a double whammy that night in Cleveland, being our first big outdoor show. In Chicago and Olympia Stadium in Detroit, everyone was closer. We got a little more used to playing outdoor stadiums by the end of the tour.

Bobby Hebb was the next act to appear. His mega-hit *Sunny* was actually the number one song in the U.S. during this August 1966 tour. The song wasn't performed until near the end of his set, but when it was, the crowd reacted as any audience would when hearing a number one hit. They all knew it and loved it.

Sunny is a laid-back pop song with an undertone of Nashville soul that could have been mistaken for a Motown release. The song was actually recorded in New York City, but Hebb is from a well-known musical family in Nashville, where he played in Roy Acuff's band as a teenager.

The audience might have expected Hebb to be more of a smooth balladeer; for instance, doing songs closer in style to The Temptations' *My Girl*, rather than influenced by Wilson Picket's *Mustang Sally*. If so, they were wrong.

Hebb destroyed this naive stereotyping by appearing in all black - including a black leather jacket. He growled his way through a number of hard-hitting, fast-paced songs, with *Sunny* being the only mellow selection in the bunch. But that description is only in comparison to the other songs.

Sunny was delivered with much more of a punch than you hear on the record. His performance was closer to one by James Brown, rather than The Temptations.

Hebb is still a force in the Nashville music scene and has an especially strong following in Germany and England. In the summer of 2004, he once again hit the top of the *Billboard Album Charts* when *Sunny* was included on the hit CD, *Night Train From Nashville.*

Bobby Hebb

We all kind of stuck together on that tour. We were a good team and it became like a family type of thing. You know, we ate the same things… The Beatles had the same things that we had.

Sunny was the number one song and that was a very fortunate thing. All the audiences knew me and the Beatles congratulated me. They liked the song. As a matter of fact, I recall all of them talking about it. When we first met, that was the first thing that they mentioned. That it was a great song and they liked it.

When we were traveling, the rest of us would play games. Like the game shows they had on television. The Ronettes came up with quite a few of them. *Password* was one of them. But the Beatles sat as a team and didn't play any of the games. If they weren't talking about different things, they were nodding – getting a little rest.

The friendliest one was Ringo. George and John were quiet. Paul and Ringo were more active.

I talked more to Ringo. I talked to Paul about photography, but I spoke to Ringo because he wanted me to do some work with them on piano. I recommended Billy Preston. I heard Billy play his version of *Sunny* and thought that he was a good musician and a fine performer. By just watching and observing, I thought Ringo was more of a businessman. He would kind of scout things and discuss them with the other fellas.

I remember Cleveland because it was a rainy night. Sam Davis, who was the A&R, (Audio & Recording), man for Mercury Records was there with his daughter. I had promised to get seats for him on the tour. They got a chance to see the show, but did not get a chance to meet the Beatles. But it was a fun thing and they were in a safe place. They were right up front, but they still didn't get hurt.

I remember wearing a black outfit. I still wear a lot of black. I also had a white one and possibly a blue one. I also had a yellow jacket which is on exhibit at The Hall of Fame in Nashville.

It was a wonderful feeling being on that stage. That was more people than I had ever performed in front of in my whole, entire life. I remember the crowd, because the way I perform is that I have to look directly over their heads. I could see something. I can see from a distance. I can't see close up. Even though I wear glasses, I still can't see close up.

We had about twenty minutes each. I don't know if we had that long, but twenty minutes sounds normal. I think I opened up with the song, *Bread*. And of course I did *Sunny*, but I can't remember what the middle songs would've been. But I always feel at home on stage and it was a wonderful experience.

Bobby Hebb and The Remains left the stage and The Cyrkle was introduced as the next act. Music fans know their big hits were *Red Rubber Ball*, (written by Paul Simon), and *Turn Down Day*, which featured a sitar. The stringed Indian instrument was a hot trend, (Raga-Rock), in 1966, thanks to the influence of George Harrison.

Music trivia fans also know The Cyrkle was the only American group ever managed by Beatles manager, Brian Epstein, (he actually co-managed with a partner, Nat Weiss). That should solve any mysteries as to why they were on the tour. It's also been reported that John Lennon came up with the name "Cyrkle," which seems to fit his knack at word-play.

The Remains returned to the stage to back-up The Ronettes, the final act before the Beatles. Since no announcement was made

concerning the members of the girl trio, it's doubtful many in the audience, (in 1966 and probably still today), knew that lead singer and namesake of the group, Ronnie Spector, was not on this tour. Her place was taken by her cousin Elaine, though Ronnie will forever be known as "the voice" of the group.

Two of The Ronettes biggest hits performed that night were *Da Doo Ron Ron* and *Be My Baby*. Their last song was the Ray Charles rave-up, *What'd I Say*. But how the trio sounded in Cleveland with Elaine instead of Ronnie will always be a mystery. The growing anticipation for the Beatles kept them from being the true focus of the crowd's attention. All eyes seemed to be on the trailer and whenever anyone pushed aside one of the curtains to peer out a window, the sound of loud screams would overpower the music. As The Ronettes left the stage, the fans knew what was coming next and filled the stadium with louder screams and chants:

"WE WANT THE BEATLES!"

INTRODUCING THE BEATLES

By 9 p.m., the night sky was made even darker by the heavy cloud layer, blocking out any hint of light from the moon and stars. Bright spotlights illuminated the stage while the Beatles' road manager and bodyguard, Mal Evans, moved their amplifiers and drums into place. As the WIXY deejays walked on to announce the evening's headliners, the screams from the crowd became one continuous roar.

Inside the trailer, the Beatles had changed into dark, double-breasted suits with flared trousers. On stage the WIXY deejays gathered behind Armstrong, (using McCartney's microphone), and Canton, (on Lennon's microphone), who had the crowd on its feet and spelling out "BEATLES."

Johnny Canton

Being the program director and having an on air show too, I was allowed to introduce the group. I had each of the other personalities introduce the front acts, like Bobby Hebb, The Ronettes and The Cyrkle, so they could go up on stage and introduce themselves and what time they were on the air.

Then it came time for the Beatles. We didn't have an intermission, so I went up on stage and introduced myself. That was me dong the "B-E-A-T-L-E-S" countdown. Then I said, "The greatest group in the world, THE BEATLES!"

Jack Armstrong

I got everybody to say, "WIXY." I was ad-libbing the whole thing. Somebody sent me a little video – a bootleg video - of me on stage and I put it in my video library. Under subject matter I wrote, "Young Kid Scared To Death," because I didn't have the foggiest idea of what I was supposed to be doing. Nobody gave me any instructions. So, after I got everyone to chant out "WIXY!" I said, "Here's the group you've been waiting to see, THE BEATLES!"

The source is unknown, but the latter part of the introduction was recorded and survives on various bootleg CD's. Over a steady roar of screams, Canton and Armstrong can both be heard shouting over the stadium's public address system:

"WHAT'S THAT SPELL?"

"BEATLES!" yelled the fans in unison.

After a few calls of, **"ARE YOU READY?!"** to build the anticipation into full-blown mania, the announcement finally came:

"All we want to do is remind you – WHO BROUGHT THE BEATLES TO CLEVELAND?"

"WIXY!" was the loud response.

"HERE THEY ARE – THE BEATLES!"

Joe Stipe
When it was time, they picked up their guitars and everybody got quiet. Then they just walked out.

All vocal chords in the stadium seemed to let loose as John, Paul, George and Ringo emerged from the trailer and quickly climbed the few steps to the stage. Thousands of flashbulbs lit the stands like mini strobe lights, and the screaming reached a volume that can only be compared to standing next to a jet taking off from nearby Hopkins Airport. In a message sent to **beatlesincleveland.com**, a young fan named Sandy remembers:

Sandy
When the Beatles emerged from that trailer, the chill down my spine was more intense than anything I'd yet been exposed to. Maybe it was all those girls SCREAMING! It's all blurry, but I can remember that George and John had matching Epiphone Casino guitars with sunburst finish, (I was then a guitar student, so I noticed that first). I guess John removed the finish from his for later use, because I remember it on the *Get Back* rooftop performance.

Jerry G. Bishop

At the concerts themselves, you couldn't tell if you were in Cleveland, Detroit or Muncie, Indiana. You could have been anywhere in the world at that time and there would have been that same kind of hysteria. There was the flashbulb thing - nonstop – and the noise. High pitched, ear splitting, and preventing them from hearing each other. It was insane, the screaming. The kids didn't care. All they cared about was seeing them and being in the same place with them. That's what it was about.

Jack Armstrong

John Lennon was standing over there next to me at the stairs with his guitar smiling at me. I put them on, they came on stage, and I went off stage - and *very happily* went off stage.

With wind gusts blowing through their long hair, Ringo stepped behind his drums while the others plugged in their guitars. After hitting a few chords and adjusting the sound coming from their amplifiers to **LOUD**, John and Paul tested their microphones:

"HELLO!" John shouted first. "HELLO, HELLO!!" they both yelled a number of times, before Paul stepped back nearer to where George was standing by the amplifiers. Straining to hear himself over the vocal hysteria raining down on them, John glanced to his right to see if his band mates were ready, and then launched into their first song, Chuck Berry's *Rock'n Roll Music*. In a message to **beatlesincleveland.com**, a dedicated fan relates what it was like for her at that moment:

Betty

I sat in the second deck, first row. When the lads came on and

my Paul started to talk, I was gone! The screams were deafening and I was chief among them. I was happily draped over the wall and my mom held my feet.

I loved it all and heard very little. But one didn't go to hear – just to be and to share. It was a delight worth losing a voice. After all, what is a voice when one can see the Beatles?

I Me Mine

The screaming from fans never let up as they bounced in time to the song. One surprise that was hoped for, but not expected, was that both the music and vocals could be heard from my seat in the upper deck. My first thought was that the Beatles sounded great. My second, as I stared at them through the binoculars my father had let me use for this special occasion, was that their faces appeared to look pink under the stage lighting. The visual is an image that has stayed with me since.

Ron Sweed

I was in the press box, my ticket is a press box ticket, and I watched the entire concert from there. Again, there was the screaming and the flashbulbs like lightening, but my first impression was that they sounded as good as the record. Live! I always thought that, even with the 1964 show in Cleveland and the two performances at the Maple Leaf Garden. I don't know how they accomplished it. Well, they accomplished it because they were doing songs where they didn't require any really major special effects. But it always struck me that they sounded as good as their singles and LP's at the time.

Wind gusts appeared as waves through the plastic lining the sides and back of the stage as they finished *Rock 'n Roll Music* and took their bows. Paul quickly moved to his microphone to sing the next song, *She's A Woman*. Obviously more of a showman than John and George, he appeared to enjoy the center stage spotlight by smiling and waving to fans in different sections throughout the stadium as he sang and played his left-handed Hofner bass guitar.

THERE'S A RIOT GOIN' ON!

For many young fans, the excitement was emotionally overwhelming. Medics were kept busy racing through the aisles with oxygen tanks and smelling salts to revive girls who had fainted and collapsed near their seats.

By the time George stepped up to sing their third song, *If I Needed Someone*, fans in the lower seating sections had started running down the aisles and were gathering by the railings that separated the box seats from the field. Fans in the upper deck sprinted to the walkways and sped down the ramps to join the others, hoping to get a closer view of the Beatles.

How much could be seen at that distance from the stage is unknown, but the Beatles did not appear to notice the growing mob and continued playing. More and more fans pushed up against the railing until a daring few jumped over and raced to the snow fence. Others poured out of the stands and within a matter of minutes or seconds, over two thousand people were pushing against the flimsy wooden barrier that separated them from their idols.

In a message on **beatlesincleveland.com**, Jon C. writes about being one of the fans who rushed onto the field. He remembers what happened next.

Jon C.

There was a row of speakers on tables, kind of on the baselines, and the song before *Day Tripper* is when people began coming out of their seats. There was a fence inside those tables and it was the first or perhaps sixth note of *Day Tripper*, when a guy jumped on the table and leaped over the fence into the infield where all the cops were. The cops chased this guy as he was bolting for the stage and he got to about the pitcher's mound before the cops got him. But that prompted the fans to push down the fence and all go to the stage.

Barry Tashian

I recently met a guy who told me he started that. His name is Mike Joyce and he's a bass player and song writer in Nashville. He said that he didn't have a ticket and had snuck into the stadium. The ushers were chasing him and he didn't have any place to go. He found himself down there along the railing and he just jumped. He jumped out onto the field and a whole bunch of people followed him.

Realizing the snow fence was not strong enough to contain the growing mob of Beatlemaniacs, Cleveland police hurried toward the stage and formed a final line of protection. Then, in a sudden surge of adrenaline, fans pushed down the fence and the race was on.

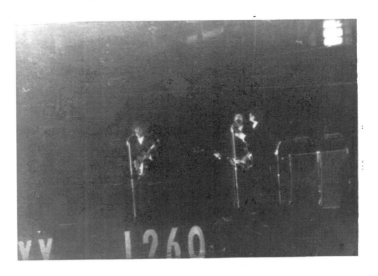

Jack Armstrong

I was standing over by the folding chairs, where the jocks and the dignitaries were sitting. And a guy walked up to me and said, (British accent), "I'm from *The London Times.* Don't you think the crowd is rather subdued?"

I said, "Well, they're so far away for openers. They're not up close to the group, but I think they're responding well. At least the people that are here."

He said, "Well, next to a Beatles crowd don't you think this is really NOT a great performance? And don't you think that this indicates the group is losing popularity?"

And I said, "I don't know. That group of people that have just jumped over the fence and are running at us seem to like them a lot."

And he went, "Oh my GOD!!" and ran behind the trailer. And we had a riot!

I Me Mine

My mindset was that I had come to see the Beatles and not the fans. I saw that they were standing by the railing and must admit feeling a bit jealous they were closer to the stage than I was – even though my parents had paid for the most expensive seats. So instead of watching the growing crowd, I aimed my binoculars back at the Beatles to watch George sing *If I Needed Someone.*

I don't remember where it was during the song, but I do recall my cousin shouting, "They've got George!"

I dropped my binoculars and saw thousands of fans running

across the field to the stage. They were moving in one large mass over the already-crushed snow fence and past the police, who appeared to have no idea how to stop them. Since we were in the upper deck and with my parents, we stayed in our seats and waited to see what would happen next.

Johnny Canton

By the end of the third song, it turned into a semi-riot. The kids started coming out of the stands. We had a snow fence and some cops, but they just ran right through that. And all of sudden, they were surrounding the stage. But of course we could see the sea of humanity coming at us.

Yeah, it was scary. I think it was a little scary for everybody, because the police had no control. In retrospect, I guess we didn't have enough cops, but I don't think you could ever have enough cops for that amount of people. We thought the fence was going to hold them back.

Bobby Hebb

I was in the dressing room and someone asked me to look. I

guess it was probably a member of The Cyrkle. I couldn't see that as a riot. I thought it was just a form of excitement, but one that had just reached a certain ultimate at that particular moment.

Jack Armstrong

The riot was outrageous. It started with about twenty or thirty people who ran right by the cops, because the cops had turned around to watch the show. Now the cops are turned around, trying to stop the other hundred and fifty that followed the twenty. And then there were a couple of thousand that followed the hundred and fifty. The cops couldn't do anything. In fact they got shoved all the way back to where the stage was.

It has been estimated that 2,500 fans ran across the muddy field as the Beatles continued to play. Seemingly unfazed by the commotion now raging only a few feet in front of them, the group kicked into the guitar-driven *Day Tripper* and were greeted by a number of fans who made it through the police line and onto the stage. Watching from her seat in the stands was Patricia D., who related her experience on **beatlesincleveland.com**:

Patricia D.

When I first saw our seats, I was upset they were so far away. I went to find someone to see if I could pay the additional $2 to sit closer. He told me to sit anywhere I wanted and if someone came along to say, "Sorry, I have the wrong seat," and move. So I did and was a lot closer, even though the Beatles were on second base – a baseball field away.

I remember a girl who had one of those beehive hairdos and within about ten minutes it was all down her face. She tore it apart screaming.

During *If I Needed Someone*, the fans were wild and leaving their seats, moving to stand near the railings. When the opening chords of *Day Tripper* started they really went wild. To this day my brother says he gets chills when he hears the opening chords to that song.

Ron Sweed

I filmed it from the press box. The real good black and white stuff is our *City Camera News* sixteen millimeter, which I now have possession of. They signed over the rights to me because it's very volatile film stock and year after year it becomes more brittle. Eventually they just destroy all that. I loaned it to NBC one time. I never gave away my eight millimeter stuff.

It first started with a guy who ran across the field. Then after that, during *Day Tripper* – BAM! That just opened the flood gates and there went everybody. We have some great footage where it looks like the *American Bandstand* show with all the kids around. There's people running back and forth, and paper confetti-like stuff being thrown in the air. And the Beatles are still singing, "Day Tripper…"

Marilyn B.

I remember the grumbling that the Beatles were so far away from everyone and it was hard to see what they looked like. All of a sudden, my girlfriend grabbed my arm and off we went like crazy people, over the rail and onto the field. We watched the police chasing people, but my girlfriend and I just stood pretty close to the stage and stared at The Fab Four. I remember thinking how tall they looked in person and how gorgeous Paul was.

Patricia D.

The fans stormed the stage, including yours truly. There were two fences – a snow fence and also a rope fence about four feet high. The snow fence was crushed down and the fans either ducked under or jumped over the rope one. I wasn't too close to the stage at first, but as fans were fainting and being carried away I got closer. I recall

being shocked that John had reddish hair. Also that their "greenish-looking" stage makeup was running.

Jack Armstrong

While the Beatles were still playing, I started to go up on stage and their bodyguard, Mal Evans, jumped in front of me. He put his hand on my chest and had this look on his face like, "I'll kill you." You know? I turned and Brian Epstein is standing there, so I said, "There's only one guy in this whole stadium that can get these idiots back in their seats and it's me."

Epstein thought about it for a second and motioned for Mal to get out of the way. So I went on stage and I'm standing next to Lennon and he's singing, *Day Tripper.*

Beatle fan John T., who earlier shared his memories of the 1964 concert at Public Hall, was also at the stadium. He recalled the scene on the field in a message to **beatlesincleveland.com.**

John T.

Suddenly a guy made a break over the fence on the third base side and dashed for the stage. At that instance, most of the cops stationed in the infield abandoned their positions to catch this one dashing dodging kid. Bingo! That seemed like a good idea as the rest of us followed the original guy's lead!

I found myself even closer to the Beatles than in '64. This time I was pressed against the stage directly in front of John. He had

shockingly auburn hair and a greenish makeup ran down all their faces as they continued to play while all this was going on around them.

One young girl wrapped her arms around Paul and then, while being pulled away, ripped the back of his suit jacket, almost splitting it in half. Another girl leaped onto Ringo's drum riser before being wrestled to the stage by police and members of the WIXY staff. At **beatlesincleveland.com**, Egdon shared his memories:

Egdon

I remember the kid grabbing Ringo's sticks and the cops, some of the oldest cops I'd ever seen, facing the Beatles and not the crowd. I also remember thinking "Uh-oh, this is bad…"

The year before in New York City, where I had been going to school, the Pope came. The NYC police, who were mostly Irish or Italian and very Catholic, probably wanted to peek at the Pope in the worst way, but they all faced the crowd and never once turned toward him. But those Cleveland guys, those real, real old cops, all stood there clapping and getting off on the Beatles while behind them brewed the teenage frenzy that eventually stopped the show.

Jack Armstrong

The cops that had been pushed back to the VIP section, two or three of them, got on stage and started pulling fellow cops out of the crowd. It was the damnedest thing I've ever seen in my life. If I live to be a hundred and fifty, which is not likely, I will never forget what I saw when I looked down into the crowd.

The stage was about throat high on most people. The first four or five rows of people were suffocating. Their tongues were out and they were off their feet. They were swaying like a snake would slither. They were swaying back and forth, but it was caused by the force of the people on the sides and behind them. Some were yelling for help, "Help me!" Some were turning blue, because they couldn't breathe! And the next fifteen rows behind them were going, "Awww – The Beatles!!" They were laughing and waving their hands and pushing.

At the front of the stage was a young fan celebrating his thirteenth birthday at the concert. He related his experience in a message to **beatlesincleveland.com**:

Bobby D.

I remember vividly that I was almost crushed to death as I was leaning on the stage while mass quantities of people were still pushing forward. The Beatles were still performing *Day Tripper*, but there were no voices to be heard. This was because of both the screaming and that we were well past the ridiculous "outdoor speaker" sound system that was spread somewhat evenly over the first and third base lines of the stadium. It was truly both surreal and somewhat "unbelievable."

Ron Sweed

At the beginning of this whole scenario you can see WIXY 1260 at the front of the stage. Eventually, you don't see it anymore. You just see a sea of people at the front of the stage.

I feared for them. I'm in the press box this whole time and I'm thinking, "How are they going to get out of this one alive?!" I mean, the Cleveland police, and I'm not trying to maintain police brutality, but they were panicking. They were just swinging their night sticks, which wasn't a pretty sight because you figure hard wood on skull at that velocity… I don't know if anyone got really harmed, but the whole worry, at least there for that moment, was to keep the Beatles in one piece.

By the end of *Day Tripper*, the area around the stage was in total chaos. The Beatles moved behind a few police officers who protected them from fans that had pulled themselves up from the mob still pressing to get close to the group.

Jerry G. Bishop

At Cleveland Municipal Stadium, the goal was to actually touch a Beatle. Cleveland, don't forget, is rock'n roll. Plus, our radio station and the others contributed to that kind of hysteria.

Jack Armstrong

John Lennon looked at me and asked, "Don't you think if we just stand here that they'll just stand there?"

"No," I said, "I think they'll crawl up on the stage and tear your clothes off." And he said, "Oh God, we can't have that!" So he turned around and pulled his guitar plug out of his amp and looked up at Ringo and said, "Ringo! We're going!"

Teen Life Magazine had journalist Bess Coleman traveling with the Beatles. Her report on the concert was reprinted in Tashian's book, *Ticket To Ride*:

Within five minutes, 5,000 fans were on the field trying to get to The Beatles. Police made a gallant effort to stop the onslaught, but they were vastly outnumbered, and the best they could do was to keep hurling a succession of people off the stage. The Beatles, who were still playing on in all this, were eventually given the order: "Run for your lives!" And, did they run!

Joe Stipe

They tore the whole fence down and everything else. I was standing right outside the trailer door with their manager and I had to run up there. Ringo couldn't get out, so we said, "Okay, just lay down and we'll catch you." We caught him and took him inside the trailer.

Ron Sweed

You see Ringo putting out his hand like he's going to shake hands. And then it's grabbed and – woosh – he's out of there! It's like a magic trick. There's Ringo. Now you see him and – boop - all of a sudden he's gone, because they pulled him off the drum platform.

It was a scary thing. Eventually you see them all go off to the side and into the trailer.

Patricia D.

The police decided to stop the concert and were pulling the

Beatles off stage. Paul appeared to be arguing with someone about it and was the last to leave. They went into their trailer dressing room, which the fans rocked.

Jack Armstrong

Ringo came off the drums and his face was so white, you couldn't see his lips. There was no color in his face. He was scared to death. Paul seemed concerned as he went by me. But Harrison was laughing! He thought it was funny! And on their way to the trailer, of course, they had their hair pulled, their shirts torn – all kinds of things happening, because the cops were just useless at that point.

Norman Wain

When they started attacking, I was in front of the stage and I was tackling the teenagers. The police signaled the Beatles that the show was over, so they ran with their guitars back to the trailer. The only thing that they had to leave on stage was Ringo's drums. But they were able to take their guitars off with them.

The Beatles ran down the steps and to the trailer. Waiting for them was Brian Epstein, who stood by the door pushing away fans until the Beatles were safely inside and he could pull the door shut behind them.

John T.

They appeared to be loving every second of it. Especially

Lennon. You could tell he must have been a hell of a mischievous kid by the look of pure joy he was getting from all of it. He couldn't have cared less and didn't even seem a bit scared of what was confronting him. Neither did George nor Paul. Ringo was just sitting up there as the kid jumped up to grab his drumsticks and then a girl came up and pulled at his hand. Eventually they had to make a mad dash to the trailer as the crowd was getting larger and more out of control. I saw Epstein going nuts pushing people out of the escape path and waving his arms for the boys to get into the trailer.

Johnny Canton

I had been standing off to the side of the trailer with Brian Epstein. We had police out there, but certainly didn't have enough to put all these people back into their seats.

Brian told me, "Johnny, this is not going to work. They're not going to perform with those people out there. And in fact, if they don't go back to their seats the show is over. I don't know what you have to do, but that's it."

The fans were now moving their focus from the stage to the trailer. Continuing his earlier message on **beatlesincleveland.com**, Jon C. related his close encounter with the group during their exit from the stage.

Jon C.

The trailer was right behind the stage, with the door that I was leaning against being on the first base side. When The Beatles came off the stage and down the stairs, they only had about twenty to twenty-five feet to the door. I remember Ringo, as soon as they entered the trailer, looking at himself in a mirror. When he looked out the window that I was looking through to see him, he closed the drapes and that was that. There must have been a bathroom just to the right as you entered the trailer.

Jane Scott

I remember when they stopped the concert. I was watching... really, I prayed. Without thinking, I just prayed, "Please, don't let this happen." I didn't want it to end this way, with the Beatles rushing away and not finishing the show. I was just feeling that it would ruin the whole thing. And they were too nice a bunch of guys to have that happen to them. But I remember how bad I felt when I saw the kids hopping over the fence.

Jack Armstrong

I grabbed the microphone and said, "Back in your seats! Get back in your seats!" I was watching this paradox of people dying and being elated, right in front of me.

I started frantically screaming, "Back up! You're killing the people in front. Back up!" And slowly but surely, the people in the back – and that's where I was aiming all this – began to move back a little bit. A couple of steps. And the people in the front collapsed from not being pushed on anymore. Most of them got up. I don't think we carted off anybody.

I worked as hard as I could to get everybody to back up and go back in their seats. At one point, Al Gates, (WIXY deejay), came on. Gates grabbed the microphone and started parodying the things I was saying. I said, "Get back in your seats or this concert is over!" And I remember Gates distinctly taking the microphone away from his lips and looking at me and saying, "This is no time for crowd psychology."

And I turned and looked at him and I said, "Shut the **** up!" Because he had not seen what I had seen. He had not seen people just about to die. He got on the stage when ninety percent of this was over and they were slowly drifting back to the stands. At any rate, he turned red in the face and I went back to saying, "Get back in your seats!" And then he went off stage and left me there again by myself, which was fine.

Ron Sweed

The Beatles are off the stage and the deejays are trying to get order somewhat restored. Normally, deejays are the ultimate of cool:

"Yeah, this is what's happenin'! The Beatles – yeah! – *I Wanna Hold Your Hand* is number one! And - yeah! – it's gonna stay up there!" You know, the ultimate cool deejays.

But here it was the antithesis of cool and laid-back. It was like, "You better sit down or they won't come back! I'm tellin'ya, they won't come back until you all sit down!" It was very hairy.

Joe Stipe

The police backed up against the mobile home and kept pushing these kids away. The cops had their wooden sticks and wouldn't let them get through. Some of these girls were screaming and hollering. They just went crazy!

They didn't hurt the trailer. We didn't let them get at it that much. We had the big sign that said Sahara Mobile Homes. That was the sign the Beatles said we had to take down, or they wouldn't come out and do the show.

When the kids got around on the back side of the trailer, they got pretty rough. We told them to back off and we'd give them the sign. It was pretty big, about twenty feet long and three feet wide, and they tore that thing to pieces. Everybody got a little piece of it.

On stage, Armstrong continued to plead with the crowd to return to their seats or the show would be cancelled. Police pulled fans out from under the stage and continued to push them back from the trailer and off the field.

Jack Armstrong

I was on stage for forty-five minutes or maybe an hour. It was a long time. Then I said, "I'm going in to talk to the Beatles. If you get out of your seats and come to this stage, this concert is over!" And I went off.

Nobody told me to do any of this. I mean, this is all stuff I HAD to do.

Johnny Canton

I also went back on stage and of course, I'm surrounded by all these people. I went on the mic and told them the show is over unless you return to your seats. And I'll be damned if they didn't go back. It was like Moses parting the Red Sea. I've never seen anything like that, nor will I ever again. They started moving back.

Jack Armstrong

I went into the trailer. I knocked first, then opened the door and went in. At this point, I didn't care who I offended. And when I went in, I had sweat through the WIXY jacket; I had sweat through the shirt, my hair… I looked like a drowned rat. Sweat was running down my face. And I didn't really even look at them. I just closed the door and caught my breath. I was breathing very hard. I caught my breath and turned and looked – and Lennon and McCartney were laughing their asses off! At me!

Johnny Canton

They were just sitting around. They thought it was a joke. They were laughing. They were pretty well protected. We had the trailer guarded pretty well.

Bess Coleman continued her report for *Teen Life Magazine*. From Tashian's book, *Ticket To Ride*:

Bess Coleman

Just behind the stage was a huge caravan, (trailer), which the boys were given as a dressing room. But, it wasn't even safe in there. I know - I was in there with them, and we were all pretty scared. Fans were beating on the windows, climbing on the roof and the thing was rocking about wildly. We sat in there for half an hour while police cleared the masses. I sat and bit my fingernails nervously while the boys just laughed and remarked that this was the best reception they'd ever had for *Day Tripper*.

Jack Armstrong

They were laughing and I said, "Alright, look, I think we can get you out of here. I don't think you should go out in the limo. There's an old Chevy parked out back and we'll find whoever owns it. You get in the Chevy, go out the gate on the left and they'll take you back to the hotel. We'll let the limo go at the same time out of the other exit. The kids will follow the limo and you'll probably be okay. Everything will be alright."

Lennon looked at me and he says, "No, we're going back on." And I said, "What?!" And he said, "We're going back on."

I said, "John, it's just gonna happen again! We don't have enough cops – it's obvious. And the cops we've got can't control these kids."

He said, and these were his exact words, he said, "Jack, you've got dangers in your business. You could get ****'ing bloody electrocuted." And I thought about that for a second and I said, "Well, you're right." And he said, "We'll go back on."

I said, "Alright. I'm going to go out and give them a strong lecture. When you're ready, come out to the foot of the stairs and I'll put you back on."

Johnny Canton

Epstein was right there by the door. So I said to him, "Well, it looks like they're going back." He opened the door and walked in and said, "Five minutes!"

Jane Scott

It didn't end, because they talked the kids back into their seats. There was one person who was able to calm them down. Jack Armstrong. He was really able to talk them back and let them know that it wouldn't go on. "Unless you went back, the show would be over." Oh yeah, sure. He got the kids off the stage.

For any Cleveland police officer who thought guarding the Beatles would be an "easy shift," the on-field riot had turned it into a nightmare assignment. Nick C. offers insight from the police point of view in an email to **beatlesincleveland.com**.

Nick C.

My father was one of the Cleveland cops. He tells the story of the crowd breaking down the snow fence and rushing through the police line. The police climbed the stage to prevent getting crushed, but my father was the last because he pushed a much older cop in front of him. He got crushed against the stage by the extreme pressure of the crowd and his uniform got ripped. With the help of several cops pulling, he finally got on stage. I remember when he got home later that evening he had a ripped uniform and blood on his elbow. He told us that he had touched Ringo's drums and acted like it was no big deal, but my brother and I were jumping up and down with excitement. He says that after everyone got back to their seats and cleared the field, there were shoes, underwear, false teeth, vomit; you name it, all over the ground.

Jack Armstrong

So I went back out and said, "The Beatles say they want to come back on. But I'm gonna tell you, if you get out of your seats – if ONE of you gets out of your seat and comes out to this stage, this is over!" I gave them that for about maybe two minutes and I took a look to the left and there was the group. I think they had different clothes on at this point. I'm not sure.

But there was Lennon laughing at me again. So I said, "Here they are – and stay in your seats - WIXY presents The Beatles!" And I got off the stage.

Sandy

They still had on those green suits and yellow shirts. The sleeves had been ripped apart when the crowd rushed the stage.

Ron Sweed

I was very surprised that they continued the concert. But I was glad they did and it's a great memory.

A REPEAT PERFORMANCE

After approximately half an hour, the field had been cleared and the Beatles were reintroduced. With the screaming reaching a fever-pitch, they opened once again with *Rock'n Roll Music*, making Cleveland the only American city to have a song played twice by the group during the same concert. But in what could be called a trade-off for this notoriety, they did not perform *Baby's In Black*, which followed *Day Tripper* at their other shows on the tour.

I Me Mine

There has been some debate over the years as to what song the Beatles actually played when they returned to the stage. I distinctly remember it being *Rock'n Roll Music*, and talking about it during the drive home that night.

It is also acknowledged by others who were there that the group repeated one song. Keith C. shared his thoughts about a repeat song in an email to **beatlesincleveland.com**.

Keith C.

What is so sad is that I wrote down each song in the order they played them, because I knew a girl back home in Kentucky that was a Beatle freak. I knew she would want to know every song and in what order they played them. That little scrap of paper has long ago been lost. I've thought about that scrap of paper many times and wonder where it could be, since I never throw away Beatle stuff. I sometimes wonder if I took the song list to her house to show her the order of the songs and maybe left the list there. Believe me it would have answered this question about the order of the songs.

Why I believe this is true is because I remember very well they repeated a song. I remember that being written on my song list and telling my friend they repeated a song when they came back on stage. Also why I believe it was *Rock and Roll Music* was that I feel that John and Paul would have said, "Let's start the concert again with a fast rocker and not the slower *Baby's in Black*."

Jack Armstrong

I'm not sure what the song was. I just remember thinking they'd done "that one" before. It really doesn't surprise me if they had played *Rock'n Roll Music* twice. Their repertoire wasn't very deep.

At the time I thought it was strange, but then I remembered thinking what the hell difference does it make? Nobody can hear them anyway. I was just glad that they were going to be on stage a little longer so the kids who didn't rush the stage could get their money's worth. After all, I don't think anyone was there to see the warm-up acts. Besides, after all the confusion, I thought it was just a miracle that the Beatles even went back on.

The debate over this piece of music trivia can be traced to a live broadcast by British deejay, Ken Douglas, who was part of the Beatles entourage and reported on Radio Caroline as an eyewitness at the Cleveland concert. His three minute recording appears on various bootleg CD's, but announces *I Feel Fine* as the first song played by the Beatles after returning to the stage.

His excitement, worry, and surprise over the riot are evident in his voice, while the background of the audio is filled with crowd noise and announcements from Armstrong and Canton for fans to clear the field and return to their seats. It is also apparent the recording has been edited in a studio for later broadcast. Following is a transcript of the report with my notes in **(bold)**:

"This is Ken Douglas reporting. Cleveland Stadium has been absolutely riots. The crowds are going berserk and they've managed to get the Beatles in safely. I'm sure the whole show's gonna stop now. The police couldn't control them. They broke the barriers and barely, luckily, managed to get the boys inside after a tremendous… a tremendous riot here." **(The recording is edited at this point)**.

"They're asking all the young people to get back in their seats. The whole place went wild here. They broke the barriers, came through the police cordon… They managed to get the Beatles off the stage. They're even all over the stage. Luckily, **(muffled sound)**, none of the Beatles were hurt. Ringo leapt from the top of the drums and into the arms of some of our officials who are traveling with us. And I'm sure that some of the equipment has been broken. We don't know if they'll carry on with the show or not. They're settling down a little now. They're being told to go back to their seats. I don't know if we, **(muffled sound)**, expected to see it be calm again."

"They're still running everywhere. The field is beginning to clear. We do hope they'll be able to get them under control and nobody else will get hurt."

(At this point, the recording is edited for an in-studio commentary. I can only assume this is also Ken Douglas, but sounds like someone else's voice).

"The show in Cleveland would stop for about twenty minutes. The crowd finally returned to their seats and the show resumed."

(The live broadcast continues. There are loud screams, another edit, and Douglas reports).

"Here they come, the Beatles again, for a second time to do their concert here this evening at Cleveland Stadium. And the crowd is, (**muffled audio**), you can hear them and I do hope they will complete their whole concert. They're under control once more. They're back in their seats." (**At this moment, the Beatles guitars can be heard in the background**).

"They are being told if they leave out of their seats and over the barrier, they will be stopping the whole concert here this evening." (**This does not match the video I've obtained of this portion of the concert. There were no announcements being made at the time the Beatles were adjusting the volume on their guitars. The deejays had already left the stage. There is another edit at this point in the broadcast**).

Ringo appears to be safe and sound. They all look fine. I don't think the Beatles got hurt. But there were a few young teenagers who were here tonight... (**Loud guitars in the background**). Here they go. They're starting their first song. The Beatles here in Cleveland Stadium!" (**The Beatles are performing *I Feel Fine* on the audio tape. There is also an edit in the recording at this point, bringing in Douglas' voice once again...**)

"Ken Douglas reporting from Cleveland Stadium this evening with the Beatles." (**The Beatles are heard for about twenty seconds playing *I Feel Fine*. Then there is another voice-over, and once again, the following does not sound like the person who identified himself as Douglas...**)

"It was a fantastic show. I must say, the crowd rushing the Beatles meant them no harm. It was just an emotional show of Beatlemania – which proves the fans still love The Beatles!" (**End of audio**).

I Me Mine

I maintain that the edits in this broadcast hide the fact that the Beatles performed *Rock'n Roll Music* for the second time. The video shows the group walking on stage after the crowd is under control

and back in their seats. Their movements on stage clearly show John as the only one singing this first song. If it really was *I Feel Fine*, George and Paul would also be seen singing.

It also doesn't make sense to repeat any one of the songs performed in what turned out to be the second portion of the show. In other words, why would they play *I Feel Fine*, (for example), after they just performed it? Logic says they opened with the same song after the break as they did to kick-off the concert. Therefore, (which is a word that makes this official), *Rock 'n Roll Music* was played twice.

Jerry G. Bishop

They were also very careful about not allowing any live music from their concerts on the air. I was on the phone reporting live from Shea Stadium. They didn't have cell phones then. And they were watching us all the time to make sure we didn't have a tape machine on while they were playing. Not that you could've heard anything. You heard the bass, basically. That's why they hated touring, especially near the end. They talked about that a lot.

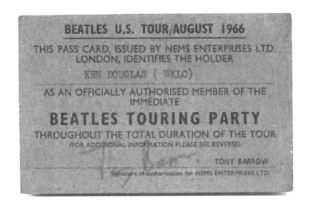

TURN ON YOUR MICROPHONE!

Fans continued screaming, shouting, crying, and fainting, but stayed near their seats as the Beatles played *I Feel Fine* – for the first and only time that evening. The reaction in the stands to the sight and sound of the group could still be called pandemonium. Many young girls were jumping and wildly screaming the name of whatever Beatle appeared to be looking in her direction. Quite often fans throughout the various seating sections would slump back in their seats and medics would run to their aid with the oxygen tanks and smelling salts. After being revived, more often than not the girls would soon be back on their feet, though a bit unsteady, and shrieking in hysterical joy.

I Me Mine

As mentioned earlier, one of the surprises of the evening was being able to actually hear the music. Most of the reviews I'd ever read of their concerts claimed that the screaming was so loud; no one could hear what the Beatles were playing. It may have been the sound system incorporating the small speakers suspended throughout the stands, or perhaps the humid, damp air kept the sound within the stadium. I won't claim to be a sound technician and give a detailed reason why, but I will emphasize that I could hear both the vocals and instruments. And in another honest assessment - they sounded great.

This was important because the next song was *Yesterday*. I had no idea how this could be performed live on stage without the string quartet and acoustic guitar that appear on the recording. There was no thought of a backing track, (previously recorded music that an artist would sing over), which is common in many concerts today.

So I was pleasantly surprised to hear their simple rendition of the song with two guitars, bass and drums. It sounded completely new and different from the record that all fans knew by heart. There was also a feeling that this would be a one shot deal. In other words, we experienced it at the show, but would not hear it that way again since at that time, the Beatles never released live recordings, (this was a decade before the *Live At The Hollywood Bowl* album). It wasn't until many years later that some of their concerts from 1966 were available on bootleg albums with this version of *Yesterday*.

Ron Sweed

What cracked me up about *Yesterday* is… I don't know if you've come to this realization, but whenever you see a film from their concerts or hear them perform it live on bootlegs, I don't think there's one time where Lennon introduces it correctly. I mean they

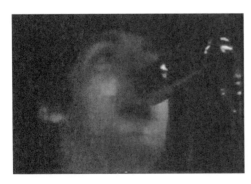

were always cracking on him because that was "Paul's big song number."

"Alright, I'd like to introduce Ringo now with his song *Yesterday*." And then Paul would finish it and John would say, "Very good, George. Thank you."

There is not a time

where Lennon doesn't goof on him for doing *Yesterday*. I know I have something where John's singing, "Yesterday, I'm not half the man I used to be. Because you see I'm now an amputee. So I believe…"

I Me Mine

As the most recorded song in history, everyone should know that *Yesterday* is a ballad. The previous songs had been rock'n roll numbers that fueled the energy and excitement of Beatlemania through the crowd. This version had the power to calm the fans - at least a bit - and the screaming seemed to subside to a lower level as many of them stayed seated and listened.

At one point during the song – and this is a memory we've had a lot of fun with in my family over the years – Paul looked up at where we were seated. My mother took the opportunity to stand up and wave. It was probably just chance, since the bright spotlights and distance should have made it impossible to see her, but Paul appeared to smile at her and waved back.

The girls seated around us swooned, screamed and jumped out of their seats to wave back. Of course my mother said his attention was directed at her and has yet to deny it whenever the subject is brought up.

Following *Yesterday*, the Beatles played *I Wanna Be Your Man*, featuring Ringo on lead vocals. This was an announcement that once again sent a fresh surge of adrenaline rushing through the stadium. Unlike in England, where the drummer was usually viewed as the "newest member" of the group,

Ringo had always been one of the most popular Beatles in America. *I Wanna Be Your Man* is an up tempo rock'n roll song and would be his only solo turn in the spotlight that evening.

Except there was a technical problem that only one person in the entire stadium could fix. That person was Ringo himself – and he forgot, (or didn't bother), to turn on his microphone.

Jack Armstrong

Ringo was so nervous. They did *I Wanna Be Your Man* and he didn't turn his microphone on.

To be honest with you, I was staring at the crowd. I was ready to hop back on that stage and unload on anybody who got out of their seats and came after them. And with all the commotion, that's probably why a lot of people didn't even notice that Ringo didn't have his mic on.

But Lennon turned around and said, "Ringo! Your mic! Turn your mic on Ringo!" And he kept on singing into a dead mic. Lennon looked at me and said, "Bloody idiot." Then he turned around again and said, "Turn your microphone on!"

The song sounded like a fast-paced instrumental with no hint of Ringo's voice. At the chorus, John and Paul both leaned into one microphone, (John's), and sang, "I wanna be your man," in harmony, just like the recording, and then it  was back to only hearing the guitars and drums. Of course it never dampened the fans' reaction as they screamed for Ringo at a volume louder than any amplifier could have carried his vocal.

Jerry G. Bishop

That's why they stopped touring, because it was not

"performing." They loved performing. But this was nothing like performing. This was just going up there and they could have easily lip-synched. They even thought about it and I remember they told me that one time. But they liked singing the words. They loved their music. And it was just developing then too, but they couldn't do that live. With all the noise they couldn't hear themselves.

The show continued with *Nowhere Man* and *Paperback Writer*. Both featured the three part harmonies of John, Paul and George. During these songs, Paul continued to wave at the crowd more than the others. This is a personal note, but it looked as if he was trying to get the fans excited enough to run at the stage again.

I Me Mine

Because we were familiar with the huge expanse of the stadium and how far we'd be seated from the stage on second base, I've already mentioned that we had come prepared with binoculars for a closer view. At one point during the show, I remember a girl seated behind us asking if she could look through Kevin's binoculars. He said yes, but before he could remove the strap from around his neck, the girl wasted no time grabbing them. The visual I still have is of him almost pulled out of his seat, with a look of being strangled on his face.

Then Paul made an announcement that caught everyone's attention. It also went a long way in changing the dynamics of how the concert would end for the fans, police – and Beatles.

A SECOND WAVE

"THIS WILL BE OUR LAST SONG TONIGHT!" Paul McCartney shouted over the roar of the crowd. That was all the incentive fans needed to attack the stage once again. There would be nothing for the police to cancel when they finished the last song, so nothing to lose except a chance to be in closer proximity to the Beatles.

Norman Wain

Some teenagers started running toward the stage. They knew the concert was close to being over. They were running toward them screaming, "I love you John! I wanna kiss you Ringo!" You know, all that kind of stuff. And the three partners, Bob Weiss, Joe Zingale and myself, were at the foot of the stage and again, we started tackling kids! It was like football, trying to keep them away from the stage.

Since launching their final summer of touring in Germany during the month of June, the Beatles had performed the same songs in the same order at each concert. The only exception was their final number, which would be either the Little Richard song, *Long Tall Sally*, or the flip side of their *Help!* single, *I'm Down*.

Both songs are full-out rockers and in later interviews Paul has said that *I'm Down* was his attempt to write in the style of Little Richard. He also claimed it took longer to compose than most Beatle

songs because he wanted to stay with the basic three chord structure, but not copy exactly what had been done before.

Whether they planned the finale in advance or made a last minute, on stage decision will never be known, but their choice offered the Cleveland audience an insight into Beatle history. The last song was one they had been playing since they were teenagers in small clubs around Liverpool.

As they sped through *Long Tall Sally*, fans poured onto the field and ran toward the stage. The outnumbered police grouped together and held them back as the Beatles ended the song, left their instruments to be protected by Mal Evans, and ran down the steps to a waiting car. John, George and Ringo wasted no time in throwing themselves into the back seat. After a few last waves from Paul, he joined them and police shut the door.

Jack Armstrong

The last song was *Long Tall Sally* and they didn't get to the end. They got within... Oh, I don't know... two phrases of the end and

the kids jumped over the fence. And this time there was no argument. As soon as they saw them coming, they pulled the guitar chords out of the amps, Ringo dashed off the drums and they ran off and got in the car. Another limo went out the other way and the kids almost turned it over. And there was nobody in it, except for the driver. It was just exactly what I had said to do earlier with the Chevy.

As a decoy maneuver, the right field gates – the same ones used by the Beatles for their arrival – had been opened during *Long Tall Sally*. It was hoped fans would assume the group would leave in that direction, making it easier for police to escort the Beatles out of the stadium at the opposite side of the outfield.

Norman Wain

What we had behind the stage were two Cadillac limousines. The first was aimed toward the exit at right field and the other at the left field exit. And the Beatles jumped into the second limousine. The first limousine started out and went in one direction. The crowd started running after that limousine, while the second limousine escaped with the stars. That's how they got out of there.

Jack Armstrong

They were not in that first limo. That's what they wanted everybody to believe. And it worked. It worked like a charm. In fact, I don't know if it was my suggestion or something they had already planned, but they used that trick a couple more times. They HAD to do that.

The maneuver worked in distracting a number of fans, but not everyone. Ira M.R., in an email to **beatlesincleveland.com**, was not fooled and knew where to run.

Ira M.R

I was nineteen and went to the concert with my little brother. I've still got the ticket stub in my safe deposit box! While it's hard to pinpoint all the songs and the stage rushing that took place, the end of the concert is burned in my memory.

I remember watching from our upper deck seats as they opened the right field gates in apparent anticipation for a quick exit. I figured what was about to happen and told my brother that it was a trick to get everyone away from the other exit. No way would they make such a public announcement about where they were going to exit. So we hustled around the huge expanse of Municipal Stadium to the LEFT Field exit.

We were not more than six feet away from the limo as it inched its way out of the stadium. Just slow enough for some young thing to throw herself on the trunk to get a better view through the rear window. The Beatles waved and smiled as police removed the girl. What a night.

With the car surrounded by fans and hardly moving, there was no opportunity for a quick getaway. The advantage of surprise had already been lost by the time the left field gates swung open like a magnet for the on field chaos. Tom M. shared his memories about the Beatles' exit in a posting on **beatlesincleveland.com**.

Tom M.

I was shocked that Paul McCartney would announce "for our last song," before playing *Long Tall Sally*, because it appeared to be a signal to the fans to rush the stage AGAIN. And, as you write, with nothing to lose, they rushed the stage. The Beatles then got into their 1962 Cadillac Limo and the right field gate was opened prematurely. It drew a thousand fans in that direction. But I could see the security men stationed behind the left field gate and the limo make a sharp left hand turn in the outfield grass. The Fab Four drove out the left field gate. It was all carefully choreographed and began when Paul said, "for our last song." I loved every minute of that night.

Working to clear an opening through the crowd, police used their nightsticks to push away fans who were desperately trying to touch the car or press their faces against the windows for a closer look. One or two officers appeared to actually be sitting on the hood of the limo as it inched its way toward the outfield gate, following more police who were leading the way.

The hysteria continued until police were able to hold back the fans long enough to open a path to the exit. The limo sped through the gates and into the Cleveland night. The Beatles had left the stadium.

Norman Wain

That's how they got out of there unscathed. They were a huge act and I know this - it established WIXY and helped to shape the future of the radio station. And of course we played on it for years after that, "The station that brought you the Beatles!" All we wanted was that buzz.

Jerry G. Bishop

I don't remember them ever walking off stage and going, "That was great!" I don't know, but I don't think so. They were always flushed because of the excitement of being out there. But it was scary being out there. They had to stop doing it.

THE FINAL NOTES

The car took the Beatles back to the hotel, where they spent the night before flying to Washington, DC the next morning for another concert. *TeenSet Magazine* Editor, Judith Sims, was with the group and her report was later republished in Barry Tashian's book, *Ticket To Ride*:

Judith Sims

Back at the hotel, finally - a bit shaken - we learned that The Beatle's limo had had to crash through an obstacle because it couldn't afford to slow down. There was an estimated $400 damage to the car, and the limousine company refused to supply vehicles to carry us to the airport the next day. Several people spent a long night on the phone making transportation arrangements. Everyone got into the act somehow, and sure enough, the next morning a bus pulled up and we left with little panic. A few fans, who promised to remain calm and quiet, were allowed to watch The Beatles depart, but they weren't able to keep their promise. The Beatles got through all right, but Alfie, (Alfie Bicknell, the Beatles regular chauffeur and for this tour, assistant road manager), fell down and cut his wrist and broke his glasses.

Before we leave Cleveland behind, I should mention the first party, (of the tour). There weren't a lot of people there, and it was rather quiet, but three Beatles showed up. John remained in his room, working on a device that made geometric patterns and designs. The gathering broke up fairly early. Ringo, who was the last Beatle to leave, had been sitting and chatting with a group of people. It was all very casual, very relaxed, and not the least bit wild. It wasn't anything like what I expected - but then, I'm not sure what I expected.

Jack Armstrong

The next day the Plain Dealer had a picture of about two or three hundred shoes piled on top of the pitcher's mound. Each was one shoe of a pair. People had lost one shoe while all this was going on in the stadium.

Ron Sweed

That was it. By 1966 I'm only 16 years old, but I've been with music's royalty. And as far as I'm concerned, they were the best musicians, songwriters and singers that there's ever been. And since then I've covered a lot of singers and a lot of concerts – even the Rolling Stones, who I like very much – but there's no comparison. It's a no-brainer.

To this day, like right now, if I look at my stereo, right on top of it is *Let It Be…Naked* and *Sgt. Pepper* that I've been playing this weekend. I just rotate the music. And it always sounds as fresh to me as it did when I was so excited about it in '64, '65 and '66.

Some people don't get it. How can we just listen to that the majority of the time? When a Beatle album would come out, that was all you would hear. I remember the summer of '67 when *Sgt. Pepper* came out. I would walk around downtown Cleveland or in Euclid, where I was raised and grew up, and you'd hear out of people's windows just a track from *Sgt. Pepper*. For months after it was released! And the same thing prior to that was in '66 with *Revolver*. That is what you'd hear everywhere.

John T.

I attended both Cleveland concerts and for anyone who doesn't "get it," all I can say is that I'm sorry you missed the excitement. Not much later, my oldest brother went to work for Belkin Productions, a concert firm out of Cleveland. Through him I have seen almost every major musical act there was to experience from 1965 through the 90's. I can honestly tell you, there was nothing compared to the magical moments of the Beatles' wild shows in Cleveland. The Beatles even stated on an old Ed Rudy interview album that Cleveland was the wildest, most out of control city they ever played in. Why do you think The Rock and Roll Hall of Fame is there – by accident? Cleveland is no accident; just ask any rock and roll band that has ever played there.

The only real danger for the Beatles in Cleveland had been from adoring fans, but it could be assumed the experience was another reason to stop touring. It was obvious from the chaos in the stadium and on stage that it was impossible to protect them in front of large crowds. Their next show in Washington, DC was protested by the Ku Klux Klan, while the August 19th concert in Memphis included a lit firecracker exploding on stage, prompting the Beatles to look at each other to see which one might have been shot. On August 29th, fifteen days after their visit to Cleveland, they performed their final concert in San Francisco.

Barry Tashian

If there is a bad memory of this tour, I think it was either the first incidence of having to play in a big stadium like Cleveland, or at the end of the tour. It was like coming off a drug or something. You forget you've been on this whirlwind for almost three weeks and then all of a sudden - boom - it's over.

At twenty-one years old, I just wasn't prepared for it. We hadn't done that much interstate touring. We had mostly toured on these day-trips out from Boston, up around New England to play colleges. You know. So here we were sitting in Los Angeles in the hotel and the tour was all over. It was just so eerie. It was really quiet. It was so like... well, nothing to do. It was strange. I actually got pretty down about it. It lasted most of the winter, I think.

I disbanded The Remains after the tour. I think part of the reason was that I was kind of discouraged. You know, because the Beatles were so, SO... They were the top of the mountain and we were mostly an unknown band across the country. There was a big gulf between us and I just kind of got discouraged. Our original drummer left the band before the tour and the music wasn't happening the way that it used to, or the way that I thought it should. I just felt like the fire was going out of what was driving my version of why we had a band. So that's kind of what happened.

Jack Armstrong:

It was an interesting experience. As I say, that was the only time I have been physically affected by rock'n roll performers. I saw them all individually since, but it wasn't the same. It just wasn't the same.

That was a very unique experience in 1966. I don't know what to say, except like I said before, I think the hand of God was in the room. They were sent here to do something – and they did it. They did a good job of it.

After boarding their flight home to England at the end of the tour, George Harrison reportedly fell back in his seat and said, "That's it. I'm not a Beatle anymore." It would be four years until his statement became a reality, but fans who were at Municipal Stadium on that not-so-typical Sunday in August will always remember when John, Paul, George and Ringo were together...

...and the Beatles were in Cleveland.

Songs Performed by The Beatles on the 1966 North American Tour:

Rock'n Roll Music
She's A Woman
If I Needed Someone
Day Tripper
Baby's In Black
I Feel Fine
Yesterday
I Wanna Be Your Man
Nowhere Man
Paperback Writer
I'm Down

For some shows, The Beatles would close with…

Long Tall Sally and not play *I'm Down*

In Cleveland, The Beatles opened with *Rock'n Roll Music* - and performed the song a second time in place of *Baby's In Black,* after fans disrupted the show for approximately thirty minutes. It is the only city in North America where the Beatles played the same song twice during a single concert.

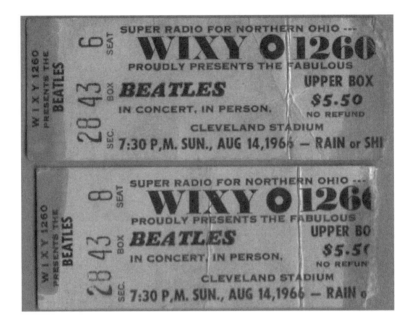

NEWSPAPER REVIEWS

Cleveland Plain Dealer
August 15, 1966

3,000 Fans Rush Stage, Force Beatles to Retreat
By Kenneth J. Moynihan

It wasn't much for the first ninety minutes or so. No one was picketing. No one seemed to care much about the disc jockeys and preliminary performers usurping the platform on second base.

The Ronettes were the last of four groups before The Beatles. They sat in the Indians' dugout in Cleveland Stadium awaiting their cue.

The Beatles arrived and the crowd was a typical Beatle crowd. Noisy. During the first two numbers, girls in the front rows climbed onto the wall separating them from the field.

It happened in the third number, and it happened first near home plate.

A boy decided to hop down into the area immediately in front of the stands, still separated from the infield and The Beatles by a snow fence and police.

A mob estimated at 3,000 followed him, and they stormed the fence. There was no chance of stopping them. Police lining the fence fell back to gather in front of the stage, then on the stage.

The Beatles kept singing. As police poked and pushed the fans away, they formed a cordon to whisk the singers backstage and into their trailer. That was guarded like the White House.

WIXY disc jockey, Al Gates, took the microphone, and kept it for the next half hour. Threats to call off the rest of the performance finally got the fans back into the stands.

As they filed off the field, the teenagers chattered excitedly.

"Wow, we'll really make the news with this!"

"My mother's going to be frantic."

Gates, at the microphone, kept pleading. No need to pep up this crowd. He was upset and his voice showed it.

When The Beatles were finally back on, Gates was trembling. "I hope I'll never go through another thing like that," he said. "I lost 10 years off my life up there."

That would bring him to about thirty-four.

Before leaving the stage, Gates asked the crowd to stay away from the right field section of the park so that The Beatles could leave safely.

Soon, two black limousines moved toward that section. The Beatles finished without a comment about the mob scene, and then the four rich Englishmen were in a limousine dashing for left field. They made it as the WIXY disc jockeys tried to save the stage and the equipment left on it.

The demonstration was the first in The Beatles' current tour. Their concerts in Chicago and Detroit were quiet.

No cotton was issued for policemen's ears here, as it had been in Chicago Friday. Some solved the noise problem by inserting bullets instead.

Stadium officials said there was "extensive" damage to the baseball infield. Tickets for The Beatles were scaled from $3.00 to $5.50.

(Author's Note: The Plain Dealer columnist confused Al Gates with Jack Armstrong and Johnny Canton).

The Cleveland Press
August 15, 1966

Beatles Show Is a Musical Fiasco
By Tony Mastroianni

Theological misgivings not withstanding, the Beatles played Cleveland in the Stadium last night. It was quite a scrimmage.

It was a replay of the Beatles' Public Hall engagement of 1964 when hysterical fans stormed the stage. This time the crowd was bigger, the terrain different but the action was the same.

The Beatles, the last of five acts on the program, came on at 9:15. Before 9:30 a charging, screaming mob brought the show to a halt and it was 9:55 before it resumed.

With two near riots in two tours, Norman Weiss of General Artists Corp. - the agency handling the English quartet in the U.S. - said that any future visit to Cleveland would depend on having enough help.

"THIS IS NOT for the protection of the Beatles, but to protect the kids," he explained.

Norman Wain of radio station WIXY, who promoted the tour here, said that all details of protection were based on recommendations from the police chief and safety director. He said that there were 150 policemen in the Stadium plus a traffic detail of 50 outside, plus, another 300 ushers.

But all of these and a snow fence around the edge of the infield were not enough to stop a crowd of several thousand when Beatlemania took over.

THE DEAFENING screams started when the Beatles came on stage, which was located at second base. The screaming continued and the fans stood up and began milling through the first two numbers - *Rock and Roll Music* and *She's A Woman*.

With *If I Need Someone* fans began storming the fence. One girl broke through, was tackled by an agile policeman as she made it as far as a spot between first and the pitcher's mound.

A young male, better at broken field running, got past the

pitcher's mound, sidestepped one officer but was brought down by a couple of more police playing the backfield.

SONG NUMBER FOUR, *Day Tripper*, found the fence flattened and police overrun. The infield was filled. Some made it to the stage and were dragged off. Police tried to re-form a line in front of the stage and failed. Policemen on stage re-grouped, reached down into the mob to drag out by the arms their trapped colleagues.

The Beatles continued singing. But with the end of that number, they left the stage and WIXY disc jockeys announced the concert would not resume until the crowd returned to the stands.

It took more than 20 minutes for the crowd to settle down. Shortly before 10 the Beatles returned to sing *I Feel Fine*.

THEY SQUEEZED in five more numbers before ending the concert at 10:10. After singing *Long Tall Sally* they jumped into a waiting limousine and drove off the field, barely ahead of a mob that came out of the stands and onto the grounds as the number ended.

As a total performance the show was ruined by a sound system that had been turned up past the discomfort level of human ears. It was a sonic fiasco, a disaster of unrestrained decibels, a monotonous cacophony of over amplified noise.

Even in an area of entertainment in which standards are hazy if not downright non-existent most of the acts were without distinction.

THE BEATLES - with experience, fame and wealth - have acquired a degree of polish and a distinctive sound. The group which preceded them, the Cyrkle, while not in the same class, stood apart from the run of long-haired groups.

The Remains, Bobby Hebb and the Ronettes all had their followings but there was little distinction or class to their offerings.

With a sound system as bad as the one in the Stadium, most of the 24,646 paying customers must have recognized most of the songs by way of vibrations. They certainly could not have made out much of the melody and even less of the lyrics.

The Cleveland Press was published daily until 1982

The Lorain Journal
August 15, 1966

Beatles Find 2nd Base Was Never Like This

The Beatles barely missed being mobbed last night as nearly 3,000 screaming teenage fans surged to the stage at Municipal Stadium.

The show was halted for about half an hour as the Beatles raced to a trailer behind the stage set up on second base. The crowd milled around the stage for about 15 minutes before returning to their seats at the prompting of police and a disc jockey.

"WE'LL STOP the concert unless you move back," the disc jockey yelled into the microphone on the stage. "Hold it, move back."

Stadium officials said the onslaught of the screaming fans caused extensive damage to the Indians' infield.

They crushed a small fence the police used to try to hold them back. About 100 or 150 policemen on duty at the stadium to control the crowd of more than 24,000 rushed to the field to restore order.

PHOTOS

92 – "Goodbye Photo," Jerry G. Bishop with The Beatles
        Autographed by Jerry G. Bishop

Cleveland Municipal Stadium
95 (left) – Beatle pennants for sale outside stadium
95 (right) - Vendor selling concert programs inside stadium
98 – Luxury house trailer behind second base

Backstage With The Beatles
99 – Beatle bed inside trailer
100 - Trailer living room with zebra couch
106 – WIXY staff with the Beatles inside luxury trailer. From left: Al Gates, John Lennon, Paul McCartney, Johnny Walters, Bobby Magic, Ringo Starr, George Harrison
108 - Back Row: John Lennon, Paul McCartney, Jack Armstrong, Johnny Canton, Ringo Starr / Front Row: Bill Clark, Jerry Brooke, George Harrison, Bob Engle
109 – Jack Armstrong with the Beatles
111 – Paul, John and Ringo Starr relax before the concert. Paul is reading *The Wall Street Journal*

113 – Official tour program purchased by the author for $1 as a souvenir while leaving the concert

Opening Acts
116 – The Remains. Barry Tashian is in upper right
118 – Bobby Hebb
119 – The Cyrkle
120 (top) – The Ronettes with Elaine instead of Ronnie Spector
120 (bottom) – Cleveland Municipal Stadium

The Concert
122 – WIXY deejays introducing the Beatles
123 – The Beatles backstage. (Author's note: This photo was sent in by a fan and is the only one in this book that can not be definitely traced to the Cleveland performance).

124 (top) – John leads the Beatles on stage
125 (left) – Ringo moves into position behind the drums
125 (right) – *Rock'n Roll Music*
126 – *She's A Woman*
128 – *If I Needed Someone*
129 – George Harrison
130 - *If I Needed Someone.* Fans are gathering behind the seat railings and only moments before rushing onto the field

The Riot
133 (left) – Fans are running toward the stage. Paul and John can be seen in the background
133 (right) – Fans on stage. Paul McCartney is seen on the right
134 – Overexcited fan jumps onto Ringo's drum riser
135 – Same fan is pulled away from Ringo
138 (left) – Paul runs to the trailer
138 (right) – Paul and Ringo (upper left), escape into the trailer
139 (left) - Brian Epstein pushes away fan from trailer
139 (right) – Brian Epstein closes trailer door
141 – Jack Armstrong (left) on stage with Cleveland's finest
142 – Fans outside the trailer
145 – Jack Armstrong on stage with police and WIXY deejays

The Show Goes On
150 – Rock'n Roll Music for a second time.
152 – Paul McCartney, *Yesterday*
153 (top) – Paul McCartney and John Lennon
153 (bottom) – Ringo Starr
154 – *I Wanna Be Your Man*
155 – John Lennon, *Nowhere Man*
157 – Paul McCartney, *Long Tall Sally*
160 – "Our last song for tonight!"
166 – Author's ticket stubs

PHOTO CREDITS

In compiling the illustrations for this book, I relied on two sources: my personal collection and the generosity of Beatle fans who wanted to share their visual memories of the Cleveland concerts. I've done my best playing "detective" in trying to locate the publications and photographers who own the rights to the originals, but with over forty years separating us from the actual events, I've run into a few dead-ends. Please be aware that every effort was made to contact the copyright holder of each photograph and give the proper acknowledgement. If there are any omissions or unintentional errors, I hope the source will accept apologies from myself and North Shore Publishing and allow us to make the proper corrections in future editions of *The Beatles In Cleveland*. Until then I offer my thanks to those who "took the shot" and for being in the right place at the right time to preserve these memories for all of us.

The magazine and book covers reproduced in this book have been in my personal Beatles collection since they were purchased *new* in 1964, 1965 and 1966. Internet searches, emails and phones calls were made to find the copyright owners, but only resulted in learning that the various publishing companies have been sold numerous times with name changes, are no longer in business, or the contacts simply don't know if they have the rights to these covers. Listed below are the titles and original publishers:

The Beatles On Broadway, Whitman Publishing Company: 18
The Best of the Beatles from Fabulous, Fleetway Publications Limited: 19
Beatles 'Round The World, Acme News Company: 21
The Beatle Book, Lancer Books: 21
A Cellarful of Noise by Brian Epstein, Pyramid Books Publications: 22
Exclusive Songs They Sing, Charlton Publications: 22
The Beatle Book of Recorded Hits, Keys Popular Song Album No. 30: 23

The Beatles In A Hard Day's Night, Dell Books: 23
The Beatles Starring In A Hard Day's Night, Dell Books: 25
The Beatles In Help! Dell Books: 26
Beatles Movie Help! 16 Magazine / Primedia, Inc.: 27
The Beatles Deluxe Guitar Album, Hansen Publications: 27
Various magazine covers: 16 Magazine, Star Time, Laugh Books, Dell
Comics: 32 / *Datebook*: 60

Jerry G. Bishop Collection / www.beatletalk.net: 89 (2 photos), 90, (2
photos), 92
Cleveland Plain Dealer: 81, 99, 100, 103
Cleveland Press: 46, 48 (2 photos), 49, 50, 52
Fan Contributions: 93, 119, 120, 123, 129 (bottom), 134, 135, 150
(bottom), 153 (bottom)
Ray Glasser / www.wixy1260.com: 102
Chuck Gunderson Collection / www.beatlestix.com: 39, 79, 150, 182
Bill Harry: Foreward, 36
Bobby Hebb / www.bobbyhebb.com: 118
Pete Howard Collection / www.postercentral.com: Cover poster
displayed at The Rock and Roll Hall of Fame and Museum,
Cleveland, OH: 75
The Lorain Journal: 96, 168
Dave Schwensen Collection: 66, 67, 70, 74, 95 (2 phtos), 96, 98, 113,
120 (2 photos), 126, 128, 129 (top), 130, 141, 142, 145, 152 (2
photos), 153 (top), 154, 155, 157 (3 photos), 160, 167, 180
Jane Scott: 91 (photo by Ron Sweed)
Ron Sweed Collection: 85 (2 photos), 86 (2 photos), 87 (2 photos),
88, 122, 124, 125 (2 photos), 133 (2 photos), 138 (2 photos), 139 (2
photos), 150 (top)
Barry Tashian / www.theremains.com: 116
WIXY / Norman Wain: 106, 108, 109, 111

CAST OF CHARACTERS:

Jack Armstrong - Known as "Your Leader," Armstrong's high energy, rapid-fire delivery made his nighttime show on WIXY Radio an instant hit when he joined the station in 1966. At five hundred words per minute, his talent behind the microphone earned him a spot in *The Guinness Book of World Records* and his own television show in Cleveland. As MC of the concert at Municipal Stadium, (with WIXY's Johnny Canton), he is credited with calming fans during the riot so the Beatles could continue their performance. As "Big Jack Armstrong," he has continued his successful career in other major cities throughout the country.

Jerry G. Bishop - As host of *The Beatles Countdown* and *On The Beatle Beat* for KYW and WKYC Radio, "Jerry G." was the most-listened to deejay on the most powerful radio station in Cleveland. He traveled with the Beatles during their 1965 and 1966 North American tours and kept listeners riveted to their radios with his nightly eyewitness accounts of Beatlemania and interviews with the group. He has continued his successful career on radio and television as Jerry G. Bishop in Chicago and San Diego.

Johnny Canton - The afternoon "drive time" deejay and program director for WIXY Radio in 1966. Along with Jack Armstrong, he was the MC for the Beatles concert at Cleveland Municipal Stadium. Continuing his broadcasting career in Minneapolis-St. Paul, Canton was inducted into the Minnesota Broadcasting Hall of Fame.

Bill Harry (Foreword) - An art college classmate of John Lennon and Stuart Sutcliffe, (original bass player for the Beatles), in Liverpool, Harry was a member of the group's inner circle from their earliest days together. He is the founder and editor of the legendary *Mersey Beat* newspaper, which included regular contributions from Lennon and Paul McCartney.

Bobby Hebb - Toured North America with the Beatles in 1966. Hebb wrote and recorded *Sunny*, which was the number one song in the country that summer and rated by Broadcast Music Incorporated, (BMI), as number 25 in its Top 100 Songs of the Century. Hebb is still a force in the Nashville music scene with an especially strong following in Germany and England. In the summer of 2004, he once again hit the top of the *Billboard Album Charts* when *Sunny* was included on the hit CD, *Night Train From Nashville*.

Harry Martin - Teamed with Specs Howard on KYW and WKYC Radio, *The Martin and Howard Show* was Cleveland's top-rated morning show from 1964 through 1967, before moving on to equal success in Detroit. Both are members of the Radio Television Broadcasters Hall of Fame of Ohio and are legendary for "saving the Beatles concert" in 1964.

Jane Scott - Truly a Cleveland legend, Scott was the celebrated rock music columnist for *The Cleveland Plain Dealer Newspaper*. In a career that spanned almost thirty five years, she covered every important rock event in the city and reported the onstage and backstage highlights to her loyal readers. A fixture on the scene well into her seventies and on a first name basis with most of the stars, two of her earliest assignments were the concerts by the Beatles in Cleveland. She was also one of the few reporters to interview the group at their hotel in 1966. Two decades later she was instrumental in bringing The Rock and Roll Hall of Fame and Museum to Cleveland.

Joe Stipe - As an employee of Sahara Mobile Homes, Stipe was responsible for the "luxury house trailer" that served as the Beatles backstage dressing room at Cleveland Stadium in 1966. He was inside the mobile home with the group before their performance.

Ron Sweed - Only fourteen years old in 1964, Sweed was already working for one of the most popular characters in the history of Cleveland television: Ghoulardi. As the resident teenager behind the scenes at Channel 8, he was admitted to the Beatles 1964 press conference and concert in Cleveland, the 1965 press conference and concerts in Toronto, and the 1966 Cleveland "informal press gathering," (where he was the only photographer), and stadium concert. For the past thirty five years he has portrayed the equally popular character of The Ghoul and is syndicated on television and radio in major markets throughout the country.

Barry Tashian - Leader of The Remains, the Boston-based group that opened all the shows for the Beatles during their 1966 North American Tour. The group also appeared on *The Ed Sullivan Show* and NBC's *Hullabaloo*. Tashian is a respected musician in Nashville and author of the book *Ticket To Ride*, which chronicles his experiences on the 1966 tour.

Norman Wain - Along with Bob Weiss and Joseph Zingale at WHK Radio, Wain is responsible for contracting the Beatles for their 1964 concert at Cleveland's Public Hall. The partners later formed the Westchester Corporation, which owned and operated WIXY Radio, and produced the Beatles performance at Cleveland's Municipal Stadium in 1966.

The Fans - They were there to witness and experience these two exciting moments in Beatle history.

ABOUT THE AUTHOR

Dave Schwensen is an award-winning humor columnist, entertainment journalist, and the author of *Comedy FAQs And Answers: How the Stand-up Biz Really Works,* and *How To Be A Working Comic: An Insider's Guide to a Career in Stand-up Comedy.* His insider's knowledge of the comedy industry was earned as Talent Coordinator for the television show, *An Evening At The Improv,* the legendary Improv Comedy Clubs in Los Angeles and New York City, and as a talent consultant for many television networks and film studios.

As a keynote speaker, seminar leader and nationally recognized comedy coach, Dave emphasizes the benefits of Good Humor in business and education. A graduate of Bowling Green State University and veteran of the fast-paced, high-pressured entertainment industry of Hollywood and New York, his message is real, experienced and simple: Good Humor can increase productivity, relieve stress, and build better relationships. This concept is also behind the business courses he designed and instructs at Cleveland State University, (yes – he really is the nutty professor!).

Tired of making his hometown a vacation spot every year, Dave relocated from Hollywood to Northern Ohio. He currently lives on the South Shore of Lake Erie, (North Coast of Ohio), with his wife, Debutante Deb, sons Chaos Kevin and Dangerous Paul, and a large dog named Snickers who is fond of eating television remote controls.

Dave Schwensen with Jerry G. Bishop
August 2005

APPENDIX

beatlesincleveland.com – Includes more memorabilia and fan memories.

beatletalk.net – Jerry G. Bishop. His CD includes interviews with the Beatles during the 1965 and 1966 North American Tours.

beatlestix.com – Chuck Gunderson. A collection of rare Beatle concert tickets and other fun memorabilia.

bobbyhebb.com – The official Bobby Hebb fan club site.

davelaughs.com – Dave Schwensen's keynotes and seminars.

northshorepublishing.com – Current and upcoming books.

postercentral.com – Pete Howard's collection of rare concert posters.

thecomedybook.com – Dave Schwensen's comedy workshops, private coaching and corporate entertainers.

theghoul.com – Ron Sweed as television's The Ghoul will have you turn blue and stay sick.

theremains.com – Barry Tashian keeps Remains fans updated. His book on the 1966 tour, *Ticket To Ride*, can be purchased here.

twelveteenmagazine.com – Celebrity interviews, concert reviews and humor columns by Dave Schwensen.

wixy1260.com – Ray Glasser keeps "The station that brought The Beatles to Cleveland" alive and well at this site.

INDEX

H

hair, 22, 24, 34, 40, 57, 58, 105, 124, 133, 134, 138, 143
Hamburg, 37
Hanson, Wendy, 72
Harris, Emmylou, 114
Harrison, George, 1, 20, 67, 69, 72, 86, 88, 89, 92, 111, 119, 138, 164, 174, 175, 176
He Said She Said, 34
headlines, 17, 24, 25, 30, 35, 39, 67
Hebb, Bobby, 28, 114, 116, 117, 118, 119, 121, 130, 172, 175, 178, 179
Help!, 21, 27, 31, 33, 34, 38, 56, 156, 178
Herman's Hermits, 26, 29, 31
Hendrix, Jimi, 27
Hey Jude, 38
Hofner bass guitar, 126
Hold On!, 26
Hopkins Airport, 43, 123
Howard Johnson's, 72
Howard, Specs, 42, 47
Hullabaloo, 114
humor, 42, 45, 58, 88, 111, 179, 180
hurt the ticket sales, 95
hysteria, 1, 42, 50, 67, 105, 124, 136, 160, 188, 190

I

I Feel Fine, 26, 38, 97, 147, 149, 150, 151, 165, 172
I Wanna Be Your Man, 153, 154, 165, 176
I'm Down, 156, 165
ice lollies, 72
If I Needed Someone, 38, 127, 129, 131, 165, 176
Indian music, 35
International Amphitheater, 71

J

The Jack Parr Show, 22
Jagger, Mick, 21

Japan, 37, 67
Jefferson Airplane, 27, 29
Jesus, 1, xiii, 36, 37, 60, 70, 71, 83
Johnson, Lyndon B., 24
Jones, Brian, 21
Joyce, Mike, 128

K

Kennedy, John F., 25, 73
King, Reverend Martin Luther, 25
The Kinks, 26, 29
KLUE, 74
Ku Klux Klan, 67, 163
KYW, 42, 49, 51, 52, 56, 57

L

Lake Erie, xi, xii, 17, 18, 19, 79, 180
last song, 52, 120, 156, 157, 159, 176
laughing, 46, 53, 58, 135, 138, 143, 145
laziest person in England, 34, 35
Led Zeppelin, 109
Lennon, Cynthia, 34
Lennon, John, 1, 20, 26, 33, 34, 35, 36, 37, 39, 45, 46, 50, 58, 60, 68, 69, 70, 91, 92, 94, 95, 97, 107, 110, 119, 121, 124, 133, 136, 139, 143, 144, 145, 152, 153, 154, 174, 175, 176, 189
Lennon, Julian, 35
Let It Be – Naked, 162
Little Richard, 26, 156
Live At The Hollywood Bowl, 152
Liverpool, 17, 18, 21, 45, 88, 90, 105, 157
Locher, Ralph, 54, 57, 58
London, 21, 31, 35, 68, 107, 129
The London Times, 129
Long Tall Sally, 52, 55, 156, 157, 158, 159, 165, 172, 176
Lorain Journal, 173
Los Angeles, 25, 34, 163
Louisville, 60, 61, 63
The Lucy Show, 23

BOOKS BY DAVE SCHWENSEN

How To Be A Working Comic:
An Insider's Guide To A Career In Stand-Up Comedy

Here's the world of comedy in one supportive, informative and enjoyable package by an author with the expertise and experience aspiring comics will benefit from. *How To Be A Working Comic* tells it like it really is: To have a career and survive, you must have an understanding of the industry - and to be a success you must be fully prepared. Provides the information and more insider's advice than any other manual, explaining how to try out comedy material; get on-stage experience; market your act to talent bookers, agents and managers; go on

the road; get on television and much, much more. Plus invaluable advice and career experience from many of today's top performers including: Drew Carey, Jeff Foxworthy, Carrot Top, Tommy Smothers, Dom Irrera, Budd Friedman, Rhonda Shear, Micky Dolenz, The Amazing Johnathan, Rhondell Sheridan and others. Foreward by Ray Romano.

"Schwensen certainly knows the ins and outs of making it in comedy. He has put his knowledge to work in *How to Be A Working Comic*, a book that shows aspiring comics everything - from how to hire an agent to how to handle road gigs." - *Chicago Tribune*

ISBN 0-8230-8814-6, paperback, 176 pages

Available from your local bookstore and online supplier.
To purchase signed copy direct, visit
www.thecomedybook.com

Comedy FAQs And Answers:
How The Stand-Up Biz REALLY Works

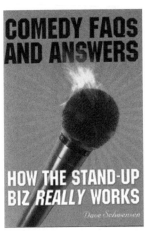

Here is the ultimate guide to surviving and thriving in the world of stand-up comedy. Some of the biggest comics in the business – including Dave Attell, Lewis Black, Brett Butler, George Carlin, Margaret Cho, Mark Curry, Jeff Foxworthy, Richard Jeni, Ray Romano, George Wallace and Weird Al Yankovic – share the lessons they learned the hard way, while club owners, talent executives, and publicists reveal what goes on behind the scenes and what it takes to succeed in the serious business of making people laugh. Written in an entertaining and informative style, *Comedy FAQ's and Answers* is a series of thoughtful questions and answers that every aspiring comedian needs to know to launch a successful career.

"FOUR STARS (Highest Rating). This is the bible for everyone and anyone who ever wanted to know just what it takes to be a successful stand-up comic. (It takes more than just being funny, that's for darn sure!) Author Dave Schwensen covers it all: This book could have easily been titled *Everything You Always Wanted To Know About Stand-Up Comedy, But Didn't Know Who To Ask*." - Todd Schwartz, CBS

"A MUST: one of the best industry insider guides on the market." - *Bookwatch Monthly*

ISBN 1-58115-411-9, paperback, 207 pages

Available from your local bookstore and online supplier.
To purchase signed copy direct, visit
www.thecomedybook.com

The Beatles In Cleveland:
Memories, Facts & Photos About The Notorious 1964 & 1966 Concerts

Hot on the success of their film *A Hard Day's Night*, the Beatles 1964 summer tour of North America filled auditoriums with screams of delight and excitement – and in some cases, full-blown hysteria. This was the setting on September 15th in Cleveland when fans stormed the stage and stopped the show. The next year, the Beatles were banned from appearing in the city.

In August 1966, the group launched their final concert tour as The Beatles, but the innocence portrayed in *A Hard Day's Night* only two years earlier was missing. Controversy raging over John Lennon's remarks about Christianity made safety more of a concern than ever before. A scheduling change brought the group back to Cleveland on August 14th for the tour's first outdoor show at Municipal Stadium. The results were the same – but on a larger scale. It was obvious they could no longer be protected in front of large audiences and the first murmurings were overheard that this would be the last tour. Go behind the scenes through eyewitness accounts, along with the backstage and on stage excitement during two of the wildest, out-of-control concerts in Beatle - and rock – history.

"The goal in Cleveland was to actually touch a Beatle." – Jerry G.

ISBN 1-58115-411-9, paperback, 192 pages

Available from your local bookstore and online supplier.
To purchase signed copy direct, visit
www.beatlesincleveland.com